HIGHLY QUALIFIED MIGRANTS
OF FIRST AND SECOND GENERATION IN
GERMAN MULTINATIONAL CORPORATIONS

Cristina Popescu

HIGHLY QUALIFIED MIGRANTS OF FIRST AND SECOND GENERATION IN GERMAN MULTINATIONAL CORPORATIONS

EBERHARD KARLS UNIVERSITÄT TÜBINGEN

TÜBINGEN LIBRARY PUBLISHING

Bibliografische Information der Deutschen Nationalbibliothek
Die Deutsche Nationalbibliothek verzeichnet diese Publikation in der Deutschen Nationalbibliografie, detaillierte bibliografische Daten sind im Internet über http://dnb.d-nb.de abrufbar.

Die Online-Version dieser Publikation ist auf dem Repositorium der Universität Tübingen frei verfügbar (Open Access).
http://hdl.handle.net/10900/133025
http://nbn-resolving.de/urn:nbn:de:bsz:21-dspace-1330256
http://dx.doi.org/10.15496/publikation-74378

Tübingen Library Publishing 2022
Universitätsbibliothek Tübingen
Wilhelmstraße 32
72074 Tübingen
druckdienste@ub.uni-tuebingen.de
https://tlp.uni-tuebingen.de

ISBN (Softcover): 978-3-946552-71-0
ISBN (PDF): 978-3-946552-72-7

Umschlaggestaltung: Sandra Binder, Universität Tübingen
Satz: Cristina Popescu
Druck und Bindung: Open Publishing GmbH
Printed in Germany

Table of Content

1. Introduction

1.1 Relevance and objectives

This PhD thesis is structured in five main chapters: introduction – in which a summary of the three articles and the applied methodological path is presented, the main part – formed by three articles focusing on the topic of highly qualified migrants of the first and second generation, and the conclusion – in which the contribution of the thesis is discussed. The subsequent introduction intends to provide an overview on the three distinct but nevertheless interrelated papers of the PhD thesis. All three PhD articles are meant to be submitted for publication to leading management journals with my PhD supervisor, Prof. Dr. Markus Pudelko. As he has contributed to varying degrees to the current versions of the articles, specifics on his contributions will also be addressed for each article.

The three distinct articles which form this paper-based dissertation focus on highly qualified migrants of the first and second generation and their individual experiences in terms of discrimination perceptions, cultural and language skills, and the interrelation between cultural identity and bridging skills.

Migrants are relocating individuals who decide due to various reasons, such as education, family reunification, work, or political turmoil, to leave their home country. International migration has steadily increased over the past decades, leading to a current peak to 272 million migrants (UN, 2020). This PhD thesis investigates the particular experiences of the subcategory of highly qualified migrants, i.e. migrants who possess at least a tertiary education degree (Iredale, 2001) as international migration research has mainly focused on investigating low skilled migrants from a macroeconomic standpoint, leading to an overrepresentation of the social experiences and challenges of low skilled migrants, and leaving in turn the experiences of highly skilled migrants largely unexplored (Hajro, Zilinskaite& Stahl, 2017). This is all the more striking as one out of four migrants to the G20 economies possesses a higher education degree (OECD, 2017). Furthermore, education has been found to play a significant role in the adaptation process of migrants, with higher education leading to a faster and better adaptation to the receiving society (Polek, van Oudenhoven & ten Berge, 2008).

The theoretical basis for this PhD thesis has been drawn from the fields of cross-cultural management, cross-cultural psychology, international migration, intercultural development, and development psychology. According to the theoretical research frameworks, highly qualified migrants are believed to bring into the employing organization important soft skills which could make them valuable strategic human resources (Hong & Minbaeva, 2017) in a multinational work context. However, a thorough and comprehensive exploration of these soft skills of migrants has hardly been undertaken in the international management literature. Thus, one important empirical undertaking of the PhD thesis was the investigation of the experiences and skills of highly qualified migrants from an individual point of view. Besides including the educational differentiating factor, drawing a generational delineation between highly qualified migrants was an additional empirical imperative for this PhD thesis. Migrants tend to go through a deep and encompassing integration process in their receiving societies, spanning from language use to identity (Nguyen & Benet-Martinez, 2007; Zane & Mak, 2003). This deep and encompassing acculturation is due to the fact that migrants have a much more permanent perspective upon their migration than other relocating individuals such as expatriates (Searle & Ward, 1990; Simon & Ruhs, 2008). Furthermore, upon looking into the individual experiences of highly qualified migrants, I concluded that the differentiation between the first generation, i.e. individuals who migrated at a later point in their life to the mainstream society (Gong, 2007), and the second generation, i.e. individuals who were raised in the mainstream society but with at least one parent from the first generation (Worbs, 2003), was of high relevance due to the roles education and generational status play in the integration and adaptation processes of migrants. Building on this, first generation migrants tend to keep their ethnic heritage constant (Fitzsimmons, 2013), while second generation migrants grow up in a highly multicultural and multilingual surrounding (Fitzsimmons, 2013; Martin & Shao, 2016). These contrasting upbringing contexts can lead to different integration patterns such as internalized cultural behaviour, language fluency and preference, or identity (Fitzsimmons, 2013). Even though the generational distinction has been included in the migrant research literature, the individual experiences of highly qualified migrants have often been left out. On the other hand, international management research acknowledges (Martin & Shao, 2016) that different up-bringing patterns as in the case of migrant generations could potentially lead to different sets of cultural and/or language skills, but these differences have often been under-researched (Martin & Shao, 2016). As a result, the oversight of individual experiences of highly qualified migrants on the one side, and the mainly undisclosed skills of specific groups of multiculturals and/or multilin-guals such as migrants on the other side, prompted the investigative efforts of this PhD thesis.

For this PhD project, Germany presented numerous benefits in terms of the data gathering context. Since Germany has known a steady but significant increase in its migrant population since the first wave of guest workers arriving in the 1950s', it presented an ideal research context from a generational stand-point. To be more specific, Germany currently has a population of 21.2 mil-lion people with a migration background (out of a total of 83.02 mil. popula-tion), out of which 10.1 million are first generation migrants, and 11.1 million are second generation migrants (Statistisches Bundesamt, 2020). Furthermore, Germany has experienced for a prolonged time a shortage of skilled workers, meaning that companies have intensively sought for highly qualified employ-ees and even resorted to recruiting from overseas in order to fill in this short-age. The considerable amount of population with a migration background, the wide encompassing generational constellations, and the employment of highly qualified immigrants constitute my main reason for choosing Germany as a fitting research framework for this PhD thesis' endeavours.

The focus of the first paper of this PhD thesis is the individual discrimi-nation perceptions of highly qualified migrants of the first and second gener-ation. Migrants are believed to experience discrimination, unemployment and/or under-employment in their receiving societies (Berry & Sabatier, 2010). Nevertheless, existing research has barely looked into the discrimination ex-periences or perceptions of highly qualified migrants in both private and pro-fessional spheres. Furthermore, each migrant generation experiences a differ-ent upbringing, education, and subsequent integration into the mainstream society. These, in turn, are likely to lead to differences in how each generation of highly qualified migrants is subject to discrimination. The first paper thus intends to contribute to existing research on migrant discrimination by focusing on how highly qualified migrants perceive discriminatory experiences in their private and professional spheres.

The second paper of the PhD thesis centres around the culture and language skills of first and second generation highly qualified migrants. Migrants are thought to possess an excellent understanding of their ethnic culture and language, which they can apply to the benefit of their employing organization (Backmann, Kanitz, Tian, Hoffmann & Hoegl, 2020). The ingrained cultural and linguistic diversity of multinational companies can lead to a plethora of operational challenges (Stahl & Tung, 2015), making highly qualified migrants ideal candidates for fulfilling roles such as cultural mediators (Backmann et al., 2020) or language translators (Kane & Levina, 2017) in the context of international business operations. However, the different upbringing and migration contexts of the first and second generation highly qualified migrants could potentially give them quite distinct cultural and language abilities. Furthermore, the cross-cultural management literature has mainly investigated the use of ethnic culture and language knowledge and its use to span cultural and linguistic barriers. Salient aspects such as generational status of the individuals performing cultural mediation tasks have in turn been left rather underexplored. Moreover, the specific *ethnic* cultural and language skills could be used as a steppingstone in the development of culture *general* and language *general* skills. These universally valid skills could be used in any given unknown cultural and linguistic setting, making them highly valuable in cross-cultural business encounters. Culture general and language general skills have seldomly been looked into (Stadler, 2017) as not only defining them, but also their investigation has been viewed as a rather daunting task (Stadler, 2017). The second paper therefore attempts to contribute to the international management research stream by investigating the differences between generations of highly qualified migrants regarding their culture and language skill development and use.

Building on the second paper, the third paper explores the interplay between identity and bridging skills of first and second generation highly qualified migrants. Since identity can mediate the use of one's cultural and language skills (Sekiguchi, 2016), the third part of this PhD thesis intends to provide important insights into the intra- and inter-generational differences of highly qualified migrants in terms of identity, and use of ethnic cultural and language skills. Due to their differing cultural and language related upbringings, first and second generation migrants subsequently internalize their ethnic heritages differently. This in turn leads to contrasting cultural behavioural patterns, language preferences, and cultural identities (Fitzsimmons, 2013). The notion of bicultural identity integration (BII; Benet-Martinez & Haritatos, 2004) has often been investigated in the cross-cultural psychology field but the interplay between identity and cultural and language skills has been mainly overseen in the international management literature. Identity being one potential factor influencing migrants or generally, multicultural and multilingual individuals, to actively use their skills (Sekiguchi, 2016), the third paper intends to provide a more in-depth overview on the interplay between cultural identity of highly qualified migrants and their cross-cultural and cross-lingual bridging abilities.

Overall, the PhD thesis expands current viewpoints by looking into the individual perceptions of discriminatory experiences, delineates between specific and general skills, and explores the interplay between identity and bridging skills, all within an inter-generational setting of highly qualified migrants.

1.2 Methodology

Highly qualified migrants' perceptions of discriminatory experiences in both private and professional spheres, their cultural and language skills, and their culture and language bridging abilities juxtaposed with their identities constituted the research focus of the three papers forming my PhD thesis. As these aspects have not yet been systematically investigated, an inductive and explorative research design was most suitable (Pratt, 2009). This inductive methodological approach allows for the exploration of the "how" and "why" questions (Pratt, 2009), thus gaining rich data (Gioia, Corley & Hamilton, 2013) from the skilled migrants' assertions of cultural identities, their use of cultural and language skills, and their experiences with discriminatory treatment. Moreover, due to the explorative characteristic of the employed research method, the development of a mid-range theory has been possible (Merton, 1968), which, although applied to a limited conceptual scope, still allows the investigation of large enough issues to be able to make a significant contribution (Eisenhardt, 1989).

The initial literature review provided first indications regarding migrants' discriminatory experiences, their cultural and language skills, and their bridging abilities. However, the research design of the PhD thesis allowed for the exploration of research paths which were previously not considered. For example, although migrants are believed to experience discrimination in their host societies, the struggles with micro-aggressions were a research avenue which was subsequently expanded. Moreover, even though migrants are known to be proficient in their ethnic culture and language, the interplay between generational status and culture general and language general skills prompted an extension of previous lines of investigation (Edmondson & McManus, 2007).

For the selection of suitable interviewees, several sampling criteria were used. First of all, highly qualified migrants working for multinational companies in Germany were contacted and subsequently selected. Here, potential interviewees from both generations were searched for since I focused on the migratory inter-generational differences and commonalities. The interviewees had a wide range of ethnical backgrounds, positions, tenure, educational specialization. This multidimensional diversity allowed for the identification of results which went beyond industry related or functional area phenomena (Eisenhardt & Graebner, 2007). Overall, 130 semi-structured interviews with highly qualified migrants were conducted, out of which 58 were with first generation, and 72 with second generation migrants. The ethnical background of the interviewees spanned 47 countries.

The interview guideline contained open-ended questions which allowed for the investigation of the interviewees' perceptions of discriminatory experiences, their use of culture and language skills, and bridging activities. Furthermore, the chosen data collection method allowed for an in-depth investigative process by using follow-up question. This in turn permitted the clarification of unclear accounts (Weiss, 1994; Witzel, 2000) and at the same time made the comparability of answers possible, as similar key aspects were inquired.

The interview protocol consisted of five main sections. The first section focused on background information regarding ethnic country, multicultural upbringing (for second generation migrants only), years of stay in Germany (for first generation migrants only), and reasons for migration (for first generation migrants only). The second section concentrated on information pertaining to the interviewees' cultural identity, identity change, language fluency, language use, language preference, cultural behaviour, and social networks. The third section was directed at asking questions pertaining to the migrants' work, tasks, and tenure. The fourth section related to the skills highly qualified migrants use in the context of a multinational company. Here, challenges stemming from their international work contexts and ways how they used their culture- and language specific and general knowledge and abilities to address these adverse challenges were discussed. The last section of the interview guideline covered aspects regarding migrants' discrimination experiences and perceptions in both private and professional sphere.

In order to achieve investigator triangulation, I conducted the first 61 interviews, while 13 Master degree students conducted the remaining 69 interviews under my close guidance and using my interview guideline. Moreover, I was able to capitalize on my own migration background when conducting my interviews, especially when addressing issues of discrimination. The 13 Master degree students who conducted the 69 interviews were extensively trained within a preparatory seminar on applied qualitative research which was individually tailored to my PhD thesis and thus held by me.

Qualitative interview studies require a rigorous data analysis process based on the coding of the interview transcripts. The interviews resulted in 1650 pages of transcripts which had to be coded. I coded all the interviews I had conducted myself, whereas the 13 Master students coded their 69 interviews. The coding results were subsequently discussed in coding sessions, allowing for the contrasting of findings, in order to decrease potential bias in the interpretation of results (Denzin, 2017). In case of differing coding, the emerging codes were intensively deliberated to reach congruence of codes. In the final analysis step, I integrated my Master students' codes with mine. Data analysis was performed with the assistance of the coding software atlas.ti, and was conducted while data were still being collected (Gioia et al., 2013; Locke, 2001).

The first step of the data analysis was undertaken by going through each passage of the interview transcripts. Each relevant passage was subsequently given a first order code. Due to the high number of first order codes, the constant comparative method was applied in order to reduce them to a feasible number. For this, reappearing labels across generations were identified and aggregated. The emerging second-order codes were aggregated in a final step of the data analysis process in which they were clustered into conceptual building blocks (Myers, 2008). Overall, the data analysis process involved a constant iteration between emerging findings and existing research, until a saturation point was reached, and no new information could have been derived from the interpretation of the data (Locke, 2001). In the following, a more detailed overview on the individual papers forming my PhD thesis is provided.

1.3 Highly qualified international migrants: perceptions of discriminatory experiences of first and second generation migrants in the private and professional sphere

The first article of the PhD thesis was accepted (after a peer-review process) and subsequently presented at the *Academy of International Business Meeting 2019 in Copenhagen*. The first draft of the paper approached the issue of microaggressions only marginally. Prof.Dr. Markus Pudelko, as a co-author, suggested instead the highlighting of microaggressions, thus improving the general argumentation of the article. Furthermore, I decided to highlight the fact that the article handles perceptions rather than concrete discrimination cases as these are difficult to prove and investigate. After various iterative rounds of writing, also based on the feedback from the conference, the present version has been included in the PhD thesis.

The focal point of this first paper was perceptions of discrimination in the private and professional sphere for highly qualified migrants. Explicit discriminatory behaviour is not only outlawed but also heavily objected to on a societal level. This has led to subtler forms of discrimination to come to the forefront (Sue, Bucceri, Lin, Nadal & Torino, 2009). For example, microaggressions in the form of derogatory statements which can have multiple meanings or interpretations (Sue, Capodilupo, Torino, Bucceri, Holder, Nadal & Esquilin, 2007) have become a tool for overcoming the sanctioning of explicit discrimination. Despite their indirect characteristics, microaggressions have also been found to have detrimental psychological effects on minority members who were confronted with such situations (Sue et al., 2007).

Moreover, migrants are known to experience discriminatory treatment in their host countries (Berry & Sabatier, 2010). Nevertheless, existing research has focused mainly on either the professional sphere (e.g. Binggeli, Dietz &

Krings, 2013) or on the private sphere (e.g. Sprietsma, 2013), but rarely on both aspects in conjunction. A generational differentiation pertaining to migrant discriminatory experiences was a further conceptual imperative. To be more specific, first generation migrants arrive in their host countries at a much later point in their lives. They are thus confronted with unknown behavioural standards and the host country's societal setting might often clash with that of the ethnic culture. This in turn means that they are often confronted with a demanding integration process. Second generation migrants on the other side enjoy a multicultural and multilingual upbringing as they have at least one parent from the first generation. As a result, their innate mainstream societal membership offers them different experiences from the first generation in the mainstream society. Apart from the generational aspect, gender also seems to play a role in how discrimination is experienced by migrants. To be more specific, by contrast to their male counterparts, female migrants are not only confronted with discriminatory issues stemming from their foreign status, but often experience a double disadvantage due to their migration background and their gender at the same time (Bobbit-Zeher, 2011; Hanewinkel, 2012). Based on this research setting, the first paper addresses the research question of ethnic discriminatory perceptions of the first and second generation highly qualified migrants, taking also other forms of discrimination into consideration.

Contrary to the results of the theoretical inquiries I had undertaken, neither the first generation nor the second generation highly qualified migrants considered themselves bluntly discriminated. Nevertheless, some notable intergenerational distinctions were possible to outline. To be more specific, the private contexts in which migrants felt disadvantaged were very much generationally constrained: first generation migrants felt at disadvantage as their foreign status put them more often in contact with local authorities, and the contact was usually suboptimal, while the second generation, who often already had the mainstream citizenship, felt disadvantaged at school, mainly by teachers. Thus, by investigating the perceptions of both first and second generation, a more comprehensive picture on the challenging realities in the private sphere of migrants was drawn.

Regarding discrimination in the professional sphere, first and second generation highly qualified migrants often gave similar accounts, i.e. neither generation perceived being openly discriminated. However, they both recollected having often been confronted with microaggressions. The microaggressions took highly indirect forms, such as irony or humour with multiple meanings, related to their migratory background. Since the professional sphere was a multinational corporate environment, employees' open hostile behaviour would have been heavily sanctioned through internal corporate mechanisms and therefore did not take place. By contrast, microaggressions were seen as an effective tool to circumvent these corporate control and sanctioning mechanisms, allowing mainstream locals to engage in more indirect forms of discriminatory behaviour. Pertaining to how these microaggressions were perceived, inter-generational differences were also in this case of relevance: second generation migrants mentioned more often being confronted with subtle equivocal derogatory statements than first generation migrants. As second generation migrants were native speakers of the mainstream language, the hidden meanings behind some assertions were far more accessible to them, by contrast to first generation migrants, who often still struggled with the mainstream language. This in turn would mean that generational status enables one the capacity to identify more clearly and better assess microaggressions.

Since the inductive methodological approach allowed for the exploration of other forms of discrimination, I found that highly qualified migrant women, regardless of their generational status, complained about gender discrimination taking much more blatant forms than ethnic microaggressions. For example, their reliability due to childcare or their technical competencies were questioned, and they often received less payment or less promotion opportunities than their male counterparts. These findings are in line with existing research on gender discrimination (Berry & Bell, 2012; Bobbit-Zeher, 2011). Although discrimination could potentially be heavily sanctioned within a corporate framework, my findings suggest that gender discrimination, although taking much more direct forms than ethnic microaggressions, was not sanctioned or even reported accordingly. Female highly qualified migrants had instead developed individual tools for coping with such disadvantageous treatments, such as higher workload in order to prove their competencies.

The first thus paper juxtaposed generations of highly qualified migrants with different forms of discrimination. This way, I have been able to contribute to existing migration research by uncovering differences in discrimination experiences and perceptions. According to my findings, both generational status and gender were relevant for this investigative undertaking: different generations sense and experience ethnic discrimination differently, especially when confronted with subtle forms of discrimination such as microaggresions, whereas gender discrimination takes a much blunter form in comparison to ethnic microaggressions. The first article therefore contributes to international migration literature by investigating the individual discrimination perceptions of highly qualified migrants. It furthermore advances research on gender and diversity in organizations by looking at different forms of discrimination in juxtaposition.

1.4　Highly qualified first and second generation migrants: how they apply their culture- and language-specific and -general skills

The second paper of the PhD thesis was accepted (after a peer review process) and subsequently presented at the *European International Business Academy Meeting 2020* and at the *Yearly Conference of International Management of the German Academic Association of Business Research 2020* (Jahrestagung der Wissenschaftlichen Kommission Internationales Management im Verband der Hochscullehrer für Betriebswirtschaft). As this article was written in co-authorship, Prof.Dr. Markus Pudelko highlighted the generational distinctions in order to make them more visible in the findings. I subsequently decided to include propositions and develop a theoretical model, and after various rounds of iterations in which the paper was improved, the current version was included in this PhD thesis.

In this second paper, I looked into the cultural and language skills of highly qualified migrants. Besides filling in skilled labour shortages in a host economy, migrants also possess certain soft skills which can be useful in an international business context (Hong & Doz, 2013). Multinational companies have an inherent cultural and language diversity due to the global characteristic of their value chain activities (Carlile, 2004; Hong, 2010). This cultural and language heterogeneity can in turn lead to conflicts, miscommunication, misunderstandings, weak team building (Amaram, 2007; Hong & Doz, 2013; Kostova & Roth, 2003), all of which can have in the end detrimental effects on the effective functioning of international business operations. Companies have tried implementing several solutions to these challenges, such as English as a corporate language, but the effectiveness of such solutions varied at best (Aichhorn & Puck, 2017). One further approach to these culture and language hurdles would be to employ individuals who have multicultural and multilingual skills.

Due to their relocation process, migrants come to experience in depth several cultures and languages. Their solid ethnic culture and language knowledge enables them the possibility to bring in at their international workplace certain soft skills which can be highly useful in dealing with ethnic subsidiary employees, or ethnic clients. However, generational status influences the development of said ethnic cultural and language skills. First generation migrants acculturate linguistically and behaviourally in their host societies at a later point in their lives (Martin & Shao, 2016). Second generation migrants on the other side, have inherent multicultural and multilingual skills due to their culturally and linguistically heterogeneous upbringing (Martin & Shao, 2016). This difference between the first and second generation in how they acquire multiple cultural and language repertoires prompted me to differentiate between generations upon exploring their culture and language skills.

Moreover, the notions of multiculturalism and multilingualism have often been researched in an ethnic-mainstream setting. However, besides their ethnic and mainstream culture and language knowledge and skills, migrants might use these as a steppingstone to develop more universal skills, i.e. culture general skills, which could be implemented in any given cross-cultural setting, and/or language general skills, which are thought to encompass competencies such as a high tolerance for ambiguities and lower language proficiencies (Cohen, Kassis-Henderson & Lecomte, 2015). Both culture general and language general skills are believed to be difficult to define and to investigate (Stadler, 2017). As a result, the second paper concentrated on the research question of how first and second generation highly qualified migrants differ in terms of their multicultural and multilingual skills, which they apply within an international business context.

According to the second paper's findings, first generation migrants possess solid ethnic skills and knowledge, which they effectively use with ethnic stakeholders. By doing so, they are able to improve work outcomes through resolving misunderstandings or explaining ethnic codes of conduct to their mainstream co-workers. Nevertheless, the fact that they migrated to their receiving country at a later stage of their lives led to an ethnic dominance in their behaviour and language, which in turn oftentimes negatively affected their own work outcomes within the mainstream work context. By contrast, second generation migrants have well balanced ethnic and mainstream culture and language skills. Consequently, they are able to effectively switch back and forth between their mainstream and ethnic culture and language, thus improving work relations between ethnic and mainstream stakeholders.

I furthermore found interesting inter-generational differences pertaining to the development and use of culture general and language general skills. Since not all first generation migrants asserted having a communication advantage in culturally unknown situations, I looked closer at the characteristics of those who did consider themselves able to overcome the challenges of culturally unknown situations. Thus, I found that those first generation migrants who had spent a considerable amount of time in their host societies developed from a certain point in time culture general skills. Language general skills were by comparison even more scarcely mentioned, suggesting that they are even more difficult to achieve. Consequently, for first generation migrants, time spent in the mainstream society seemed to be an important factor in the development of culture general and language general skills. Second generation migrants on the other hand, asserted to have possessed these skills from early on, and noticed them for example during their studies abroad or within their social networks. I therefore proposed that the multicultural and multilingual upbringing second generation migrants receive provides them with innate culture general and language general skills, whereas first generation migrants need time to achieve them.

The second paper contributes to existing cross-cultural management research through a comprehensive overview on the culture and language skills of highly migrants. By drawing a generational distinction line, I found particularities on how each generation develops and implements their ethnic culture and language skills. Although migrants bring in valuable soft skills, their generational status shapes their ethnic culture and language proficiency and subsequently the way in which these skills are implemented in an international business context. Furthermore, I went beyond the ethnic-mainstream setting and established certain particularities in terms of generational status regarding the less researched concepts of culture general and language general skills. These skills have been investigated more seldom by contrast to the ethnic flip side of the coin as they are difficult to pinpoint and thus examine. Nevertheless, I managed to bring in a more detailed overview on these universally valid skills by displaying potential disparities in their development, and their implementation in a multinational corporate context.

1.5 The impact of cultural identity on cross-cultural and cross-lingual bridging skills of highly qualified migrants

The third paper of the PhD thesis was accepted (after a peer review process) and was subsequently presented at the *European Academy of Management Conference 2021,* and will be also presented at the forthcoming *Academy of Management Conference 2021.* Being an article written in co-authorship, Prof.Dr. Markus Pudelko made valuable improvements in the argumentation of the paper, thus strengthening its academic content. After various rounds of iteration of writing, the current version of the article was included in this PhD thesis.

The third paper of the PhD thesis explores the impact of cultural identity on bridging abilities of highly qualified migrants. The cultural and language abilities of highly qualified migrants have been an underexplored topic in international migration literature. However, cross-cultural management research acknowledges that migrants bring with them valuable soft skills which can be useful for multinational companies (Hong & Minbaeva, 2017) but the antecedents which enable bridging activities have often been left out. As a result, the investigation of highly qualified migrants as a specific category of individuals who are able to perform cultural and language bridging activities presents a shortcoming.

In my research endeavours, I considered a generational distinction to be of importance upon looking into the bridging activities that migrants performed. To be more specific, first generation migrants are often believed to keep a strong connection to their ethnic heritage, meaning that they tend to keep their ethnic identity (Fitzsimmons, 2013) or a preference for their ethnic language. Second generation migrants, on the other side, enjoy a multicultural and multilingual upbringing. They are believed to have a well-balanced connection with both ethnic and mainstream cultures and languages. As a result, there appears to be a general agreement that second generation migrants have a plural identity (Fitzsimmons, 2013). In terms of bridging abilities of migrants, their cultural identity is believed to play a significant role in the implementation of their culture and language skills (Sekiguchi, 2016).

Furthermore, education plays an important role on the integration process of migrants in the sense that a higher education has been found to lead to a better and faster acculturation in the receiving society (Polek et al., 2008). Taking the generational distinctions and educational aspect into consideration, the third article intends to investigate how the first and the second generation of highly qualified migrants differ from each other in the impact of their cultural identity on their cross-cultural and cross-lingual bridging skills.

In line with existing research (Fitzsimmons, 2013), I have found that first generation migrants tend to keep their ethnic culture and language dominant. Although they were able to effectively use these ethnic skills with ethnic stakeholders, their bridging abilities were sometimes limited by their lack of an internalization or knowledge of the mainstream culture and language. However, contrary to existing research, I found that first generation highly qualified migrants can also develop plural and more complex forms of cultural identity upon a prolonged stay in their host societies. This finding runs counter to existing beliefs that first generation migrants will remain anchored in their ethnic identity. Many of my first generation respondents who asserted having a plural identity, already had distanced themselves from their ethnic culture but had kept a language connection to their home country. This in turn impacted their bridging abilities, in the sense that they were even less skilled bridging agents than their first generation counterparts with an ethnic identity due to their dissociation from their ethnic culture.

Secondly, I have also found interesting particularities pertaining to the second generation of highly qualified migrants. As expected, the majority of my second generation respondents had a plural identity. Due to their multicultural and multilingual upbringing, they were equally immersed in both ethnic and mainstream cultures and languages. They were thus ideal bridging agents in a multinational work context as they had a well-balanced embeddedness in both ethnic and mainstream culture and language. Nevertheless, I have also had second generation migrants who already saw themselves as exclusive members of the mainstream society, i.e. they had a mainstream identity. This finding suggests, that it might take less than three generations until migrants develop a mainstream identity, running counter to common inter-generational migrant conceptions (Fitzsimmons, 2013). Upon a closer examination of the characteristics of these second generation respondents, I have noticed that the educational and social advancement seems to have played an important role in second generation migrants' cultural identity development. Being mainly the offspring of the low skilled generation of guest workers, these second generation respondents were able to overcome the social and educational niches of their parents and reach a higher education and according higher social status in the mainstream society. Moreover, similar to the first generation with a plural identity, second generation migrants with a mainstream identity had reduced bridging abilities due to their mainstream orientation. The fact that they considered themselves full members of only the mainstream culture and society led to fulfilling bridging activities only on an irregular basis and to a detachment from their ethnic cultural heritage.

The third paper thus focused on the interplay between identity and cross-cultural and cross-lingual bridging skills of highly qualified migrants. I have found generational status, time spent in mainstream society, and educational advancement to play a role in the cultural identity development of migrants. This in turn impacted the bridging skills and activities that these migrants undertook within their international business framework. By drawing these investigating lines, I was able to deliver a more comprehensive overview on the interplay between cultural identity and bridging skills, thus adding to the existing cross-cultural management investigative undertakings.

2. Highly skilled qualified international migrants:

perceptions of discriminatory experiences of first and second generation migrants in the private and professional sphere[1]

Abstract

Based on 130 semi-structured interviews with highly qualified migrants of the first and second generation, we explore their perceptions of discriminatory experiences in both private and professional spheres. We find that highly qualified migrants of both generations consider themselves hardly affected by discrimination, a finding that stands in stark contrast to previous studies and widely held beliefs. Despite this encouraging assessment, microaggressions in the form of ambiguous segregating statements or behaviour is still a regular occurrence in daily life situations and within organisations. We also reveal that gender-based discrimination appears to take more explicit forms than ethnic-based discrimination.

---

[1] An earlier version of this article was accepted and presented at the Academy of International Business Meeting 2019.

2.1 Introduction

Global migration has become an unquestionable reality of today's societies, for emigration and immigration countries alike. Castles, Haas & Miller (2013:5) speak about our times as "the age of migration", in which not only those with specific migration experiences are affected by migration and its effects, but all members of all societies. As such, migration becomes an "universal experience" (Castles et al., 2013: 5). According to the UN, as of 2019, *international migration* has encompassed around 272 million people (UN, 2020). However, formal definitions of international migration differ substantially across countries, making also cross-country comparisons a challenging endeavour. Definitions usually vary along multiple questions, such as whether the classification is formally ascribed or self-selected; whether the migration status can be also hereditary and therefore independent of own migration experiences; or how children who have one foreign and one local parent are considered (Schewel, 2020). We regard migrants, for the purpose of this paper, as having an ascribed status which covers own migration experiences (first generation) as well as the offspring (second generation) of families with at least one migrant parent. International migration continues to be a major issue for sending countries as well as receiving societies, a fact well reflected in the political and popular debates on the increasing movement of refugees and other categories of relocating individuals, such as (highly) qualified migrants. Our study looks at international migration from the perspective of a receiving country, specifically Germany.

As most migration studies focus, explicitly or implicitly, on low skilled migrants, the experiences of highly skilled migrants have been largely left unaddressed (Kofman & Raghuram, 2006). This is quite striking considering that more than one in four migrants moving into the G20 economies holds at least a tertiary education degree (OECD, 2017). Initial prior research already suggested that higher educational levels should be associated with lower adaptation stress of migrants (Berry, 1997) and with a higher degree of identification with the host country (Polek, van Oudenhoven & ten Berge, 2008). Therefore, particularly when investigating the post-migratory experiences of integrating migrants into their receiving societies, it conceptually makes sense to *differentiate between the educational levels* of migrants. It is also advisable to particularly look into the neglected group of *highly qualified migrants*, not least because of their significance for the economies of the receiving countries. The present study therefore differentiates between the educational level of migrants and focuses on the sub-group of highly qualified migrants.

When it comes to the integration of (highly qualified) migrants into the receiving society, we furthermore argue that a *generational distinction* is a conceptual and practical imperative. *First generation migrants*, who can be defined as those migrants who were born in a different country from the receiving country (Gong, 2007), are confronted with a new culture to which they need to adapt and (frequently) with an unknown language they need to learn. By contrast, *second generation migrants*, who were born in the receiving country but have at least one parent from the first generation of migrants (Worbs, 2003), are raised from birth onwards into a multicultural and multilingual environment. Given these entirely different upbringing contexts, it conceptually makes fully sense to differentiate between these generations, particularly when studying integration challenges or experiences of migrants. So far, however, not many migration studies, at least not within business research (e.g., Carlsson, 2010), have made this important distinction between migrant generations. By contrast, in this study we present and analyse our findings for both generations separately.

Even though migration by highly qualified individuals has a positive impact on the host countries (OECD, 2017), this international mobile workforce has been confronted with the issue of *discrimination* (Al Ariss, Vassilopoulou, Özbilgin & Game, 2013). Given the increasing anti-immigration sentiments across many Western countries, we consider discrimination of migrants to be a highly timely and important topic which deserves scholarly attention, both for conceptual reasons and to provide assistance in finding practical solutions to a poignant social problem.

Discrimination of migrants has been reported for various situations of their *private and professional lives*. In the *private sphere*, discrimination of migrants has been found to take place at school (Worbs, 2003), when searching for housing (Berry & Bell, 2012), or in their day-to-day social interaction with members of the mainstream population (Vivero & Jenkins, 1999). Regarding the *professional sphere*, migrants have often been described as over-proportionally unemployed or underemployed (Al Ariss & Crowley-Henry, 2013), suggesting discrimination when searching for employment (Carlsson & Rooth,

2008). Other instances of discrimination relate to interactions at the workplace with supervisors and colleagues (Tuchick Hakak & Al Ariss, 2013). To the best of our knowledge, previous studies have focused so far on discriminatory treatment in either the private or the professional sphere, but not conjunctly and comparatively. This study attempts to be more comprehensive, investigating both spheres and strictly separating between them in the presentation and analysis of data. Moreover, since cases of explicit and unequivocal discrimination are not always reported and proven, we focused on the perceptions of highly skilled migrants regarding potential discriminatory treatment.

In our literature review on discriminatory experiences of migrants, we noticed the already mentioned oversight of the migration literature in investigating such experiences of highly qualified migrants (Silberman, Alba & Fournier, 2007). Empirically, we consider that highly qualified migrants present a rather important group for migration research, especially given that they form an important part of the workforce of the receiving economies (Guo & Al Ariss, 2015). Furthermore, this is an important research gap, as highly skilled migrants have a significantly higher social and professional status, which should have clear implications on any discrimination experiences.

Ultimately, while this study is about (or at least: originated exclusively as a study of) perceptions of migrants regarding *ethnic-based discrimination*, it also is of importance not to consider this particular form of discrimination in isolation. Instead, meaningful information can be provided by comparing the relevance of ethnic-based discrimination with other possible forms of discrimination, such as *gender-based discrimination*.

Based on the above outlined considerations, it is the purpose of this study to address the following research question: *what are first and second generation highly qualified migrants' perceptions of ethnic discriminatory experiences in their private and professional lives, compared also to other forms of discrimination?*

Due to the complexity of these interrelated aspects, we considered an explorative and inductive approach best suited (Pratt, 2009). As a result, we designed a qualitative, interview-based study which is particularly useful for gaining an in-depth insight in individual experiences (Gioia, Corley & Hamilton, 2013). Through a systematic qualitative analysis of 130 semi-structured interviews with highly skilled first and second generation migrants, this study provides a comprehensive picture and in-depth understanding of their discriminatory experiences in both the professional and the private spheres. In doing so, it advances research on (highly skilled) migrants and on perceptions of discrimination by revealing different discriminatory experiences according to generation, according to the (private and professional) spheres, and by putting ethnic-based discrimination into perspective, in particular when comparing it with gender-based discrimination. Furthermore, we develop practical recommendations for managers to create an inclusive workplace.

2.2 Theoretical Background

2.2.1 Integration of (highly qualified) migrants into the receiving culture

Most of the initial literature on migration within and to Europe (e.g., Vedder, Sam & Liebkind, 2007; Simon & Ruhs, 2008) or to the US (Martin, 2008) has focused on *unskilled migrants* (for example from Southern Europe and North Africa to North and Central Europe, or from Mexico to the US) and their (often problematic) integration into their receiving country. Unskilled migrants predominantly come from low social classes in their home countries (Crul & Doomernik, 2003; Thomson & Crul, 2007) and undertake in their host countries unskilled jobs such as low wage labor in manufacturing, construction and agriculture (Portes & Fernandes-Kelly, 2008), or domestic work (Berry & Bell, 2012). By contrast, more recent literature described the influx of *highly qualified migrants* in the last decades. This highly qualified mobile workforce usually has a tertiary education (Iredale, 2001) and occupies jobs in engineering, programming, the medical field (Portes & Fernandez-Kelly, 2008), or has managerial positions (Mattoo, Neagu & Özden, 2008). Highly skilled migrants differ from unskilled newcomers not only in terms of their skills and positions, but also regarding adaptation and integration in the receiving society. Higher education has been found to be associated with lower integration stress (Beiser et al., 1988) and better adjustment to the host culture (Polek et al., 2008). Therefore, migrants with a high educational level and, accordingly, higher socio-economic status, tend to also identify themselves more with their receiving society (Recchi & Nebe, 2003). Furthermore, the level of education and mainstream language fluency are highly interlinked as higher educated migrants tend to closely adopt the host country's language (Yağmur & van der Vijver, 2012).

Highly skilled migrants should not only be differentiated from unskilled immigrants in terms of adaptation processes, but also from a related, third group, *self-initiated expatriates*. Since both categories imply a skilled and internationally mobile workforce, the literature has frequently used these terms interchangeably and inconsistently (Al Ariss, 2010), leading to an ambiguous distinction between both concepts (Al Ariss & Crowley-Henry, 2013; Guo & Al Ariss, 2015). However, given substantially different adaptation and assimilation processes, the differentiation between skilled migrants and self-initiated expatriates is far from being trivial. Firstly, even though self-initiated expatriates stay longer than organizational expatriates in their receiving country, they still tend to relocate again after ten years of stay (Tharenou, 2015). Building on this, by contrast to migrants, who have a more permanent relocation mindset (Al Ariss & Crowley-Henry, 2013), self-initiated expatriates do begin to consider a new relocation at a given point (Cerdin & Selmer, 2014; Tharenou, 2010). Secondly, self-initiated expatriates might adapt to the mainstream society for a short period of time, but they tend to keep a strong connection to their ethnic values and norms (Cerdin, Diné, & Brewster, 2014). Migrants on the other hand, who usually view the receiving country as their new home country, are likely to choose a more encompassing, deeper-going psychological adjustment which also involves a change in norms and values (Searle & Ward, 1990).

We argue that an investigation of highly skilled migrants and their experiences into their receiving cultures should also consider the *generational differences* as relevant for their juxtaposition. Adjustment to another country is a complex process which encompasses elements such as language acquisition, behavioral integration, and possibly even identity change (Bakker, van der Zee & van Oudenhoven, 2006; Simon & Ruhs, 2008). Age of migration, i.e.the age of the arrival in the new country, significantly impacts the "assimilation, acculturation, and economic success" (Berg & Eckstein, 2009: 3) of migrants. As such, a distinction between first and second generation migrants is needed. The *first generation of migrants* is defined by migration research as those migrants being born in a country different from the receiving or so-called mainstream country (Gong, 2007). By contrast, the *second-generation of migrants* is defined as the offspring of first generation migrants who is born and grows up in the mainstream society (Heath, Rothon & Kilpi, 2008; Worbs, 2003). This generational distinctness is important as the first generation tends to keep their ethnic language, i.e. home country language, as dominant (Yağmur & van de Vijver, 2012), whereas the second generation usually grows up bilingually (Fitzsimmons, 2013). In addition, the differing migrant generations also experience contrasting identity formation processes. The first generation tends to identify more with the ethnic country, and the second generation with both ethnic and mainstream cultures (Fitzsimmons, 2013). Due to their more comprehensive assimilation to the mainstream society, second generation migrants also tend to reach higher educational levels than their parents (Diehl & Koenig, 2009). Therefore, they are often able to leave the social and economic niches (Diehl & Koenig, 2009) of their parents and reach a higher socio-economic status in the mainstream society (Rumbaut, 2004).

2.2.2 Discrimination of (highly qualified) migrants

Europe has recently experienced a rise in popularity of anti-immigration political views from far-right wing parties (for example, Austria, France, Hungary). Also, the UK's decision to leave the EU or the USA's adoption of strict anti-immigration policies, have generated an increase in negative views on migrants worldwide. These recent political developments reveal an increasing intolerance towards foreign ethnicities both in Europe (European Commission against racism and intolerance, 2017), and in the USA (Almeida, Biello, Pedraza, Wintner & Viruell-Fuentes, 2016). Therefore, the issue of discrimination against migrants has become (again) a salient and particularly timely topic, in the migration literature and beyond. Migrants have also often been described in the past as discriminated against (Berry & Sabatier, 2010), oppressed (Essers, Benschop & Doorewaard, 2010), and not being able to overcome societal barriers in their host country (Al Ariss, Koall, Özbilgin & Suutari, 2012).

Discrimination has been defined in this context as "unfair behavioral biases" (Dipboye & Colella, 2005:2), when superficial characteristics such as skin color are used as a reason to "restrict individuals' access to the available economic, political, and social opportunities for advancement" (D'Amico, 1987: 310). This discriminatory treatment can be based on a variety of personal characteristics such as religion, age, gender, ethnicity, or sexual orientation (Young, Shoss, Farmer & Harris, 2017). While open discriminatory treatment might in many countries be on decline, also due to an increasing societal awareness and the adoption of legislation that sanctions discriminatory behaviour and actions, more subtle forms of discrimination are on the rise (Basford, Offermann & Behrend, 2014; Sue, Bucceri, Lin, Nadal & Torino, 2009). These might include uncivility, which can be difficult to prove and hence sanction (Binggeli, Dietz & Krings, 2013; Cortina, 2008; Deitch, Barsky, Butz, Chan, Brief & Badley, 2003) or microaggressions, which are ingenious and subtle indignities meant to put down people of colour (Pierce, 1970; Sue, Capodilupo, Torino, Bucceri, Holder, Nadal & Esquilin, 2007) or other systematically disadvantaged groups (McTernan, 2018). Specifically, microaggressions can take mainly the form of microassaults (e.g. derogatory name calling), microinsults (e.g. rude or insensitive communication meant to demean a person's ethnicity or race), and microinvalidations (e.g. communication that excludes or nullifies the experiences, thoughts and feelings of minorities) (Sue et al., 2007). Furthermore, subtle forms of discrimination are usually omitted from research since proving them can be a rather demanding task (Sue et al., 2007)

To our knowledge, research has not yet differentiated between discriminatory experiences in various contexts that gradually go from less contact with members of the mainstream population, such as with public officials or when searching for housing, to daily prolonged interaction with members of the mainstream society, such as the workplace. By contrast, we mainly found research focusing either on one single life context, such as school (e.g. Fernandez-Kelly, 2008; Sprietsma, 2013), housing (e.g. Massey & Lundy, 2001), the workplace (e.g. Binggeli et.al., 2013), or general discriminatory experiences (Van Laer & Janssens, 2011).

Based on the literature we reviewed, we distinguish between perceptions of discriminatory treatment towards migrants in two main domains of life, the *private* and the *professional sphere*. In terms of their private life, many migrants have, for example, encountered discriminatory treatment at school, in the form of mobbing by classmates and low expectations or grades from teachers (Sprietsma, 2013). Other prejudiced experiences in the private sphere relate to having difficulties finding housing (Valentine, Silver & Twigg, 1999). Furthermore, some experience discrimination for appearing to members of the receiving society as too ethnic and too much in contrast to the mainstream society (Benet-Martinez & Haritatos, 2005). In addition, even the opposite reason might lead to discrimination, i.e. when members of the mainstream society find migrants too mainstream, because of not showing the expected ethnic behaviour (Benet-Martinez & Haritatos, 2005).

Most of the literature on migrant discrimination focuses on discriminatory treatment in the professional sphere, making the discriminatory experiences from the private sphere rather overlooked in comparison. As such, research has shown that migrants are regularly confronted with racial or ethnic discrimination when searching for a job (Almeida et.al., 2016; Bertrand & Mullainathan, 2004; Derous, Peppermans & Ryan, 2017; Pager & Western, 2012) or, after being employed, in the form of less payment or less career advancement opportunities (Hajro, Zilinskaite & Stahl, 2017; Turchick Hakak & Al Ariss, 2013). Female migrants might, additionally to racial ethnic discrimination, be also confronted with gender discrimination at work (Bobbit-Zeher, 2011; Cortina, 2008 Hanewinkel, 2012).

Most of the abovementioned findings have been established with lower skilled migrant populations. Consequently, there appears a clear prevalence of research on *discrimination of low skilled migrants*, in particular regarding the professional domain (e.g., Bovenkerk, Gras & Ramsoedh, 1994; Crul & Doomernik, 2003; Silberman et al., 2007). By contrast, the investigation of *discriminatory treatment of highly skilled migrants* at the workplace is significantly less prominent (exceptions are Al Ariss et al., 2013; Carlsson & Rooth, 2007; Van Laer & Janssens, 2011). This evident bias (Al Ariss, Cascio & Paauwe, 2014) against research on discrimination of highly skilled migrants might astonish, given that they form a significant part of the workforce in today's developed societies (Guo & Al Ariss, 2015; Kofman & Raghuram, 2006). Nevertheless, the scant research on discrimination of highly skilled migrants established that in comparison to low skilled migrants, they appear to experience less discrimination (Carlsson & Rooth, 2008) and if so, more subtle discrimination (Van Laer & Janssens, 2011). And even though they might have reached a relatively high level of socio-economic status, highly skilled migrants still belong to groups that are negatively stereotyped (Al Ariss et al., 2013). Furthermore, the second generation benefited from the same educational opportunities as members of the mainstream population and speak the mainstream language as their native language. Nevertheless, ethnic-based job discrimination has been described as a widespread issue among second generation migrants (Carlsson, 2010; Crul & Doomernik, 2003; Hanewinkel, 2012; Kaas & Manger, 2011).

So far only a few studies on discrimination of highly skilled migrants have been undertaken and again, only a handful of other investigations considered discrimination between generations. Both aspects were usually explored from within migration research but scarcely by (international) business research scholars. However, to the best of our knowledge, a comprehensive investigation that looked at discrimination experiences from a generational standpoint of highly skilled migrants is not available, neither from migration research, nor from business research. This is a surprising research gap, given the high (and growing) percentages of highly skilled employees with a migration background in the workforce of today's advanced economies and the continuously increasing number of second generation migrants (Van Oudenhoven, Ward & Masgoret, 2006). We hold that this research gap is of major conceptual significance, mainly due to the substantial differences in the upbringing of first and second-generation migrants and, as we found, their different perceptions of discriminatory experiences to which organizations need to respond. It is this latter aspect which suggests also important practical implications, equally necessitating the investigation of this research gap. After all, organizations and individual managers will have to address the distinct forms of discrimination in specific ways, in order to assure the optimal utilization of significant parts of the working population (not to mention assuring the fair treatment of employees). Furthermore, we intend to break down potentially different discriminatory perceptions between the migrant generations also according to various life contexts. To be more specific, we looked into the perceptions of discriminatory treatment for both first and second generation, and also in their respective private and professional spheres.

It is ultimately also of interest that studies so far have clearly separated according to the type of discrimination, such as ethnic- (Guo & Al Ariss, 2015) or gender-based discrimination (Bobbit-Zeher, 2011). We consider this approach to recreate only partially the realities of female migrants, as women are often confronted with a twofold detriment: foreign ethnicity and gender (Hanewinkel, 2012). This means that in addition to their foreign status and the subsequent disadvantages, women are confronted with additional societal and career barriers (Guo & Al Ariss, 2015). These can take the form of underemployment (Berry & Bell, 2012), less payment by contrast to their male colleagues (Hamilton, Alagna, King & Lloyd, 1987), and less job promotions, partly because of issues of dependability due to childcare (Ortiz & Roscigno,

2009). We thus consider the comparison of the impact of different forms of discrimination to be of conceptual and practical importance.

To conclude, it is the objective of this study to exploratively investigate *the first and second generation highly qualified migrants' perceptions of ethnic discriminatory experiences in their private and professional lives, considering also other forms of discrimination in comparison.*

2.3 Methodology

2.3.1 Research design

We employed an explorative, inductive approach in our study as we were first and foremost interested in obtaining an in-depth understanding of the migrants' experiences and perceptions of discrimination (Birkinshaw, Brannen & Tung, 2011; Pratt, 2009). By contrast, a deductive, theory testing approach would have been less suitable, given that the discrimination in the case of highly skilled migrants in the private and professional sphere, specifically taking into account generational differences, has hardly been systematically investigated. In the tradition of grounded theory (Glaser & Strauss, 1967; Strauss & Corbin, 1998), we therefore started out with the broad objective of examining discrimination perceptions from the migrants' perspective. Although the mainly sociological literature, namely on migration and discrimination, provided us with some initial clues, we were entirely open about what our interviewees were going to relate on how they experienced discrimination. After various rounds of iterations between data generation, data analysis and literature review, we noticed the relevance of gender-based discrimination in direct comparison to ethnic-based discrimination. This observation prompted us to expand our research beyond our original scope and extend our conceptualization into lines of thoughts we had previously not considered (Edmondson & McManus, 2007).

2.3.2 Research setting

In order to exclude the influence of national institutional differences in educational systems, labour market regulations, and discrimination and integration policies (Crul & Vermeulen, 2003), we kept the country of investigation constant. In the context of our research, Germany is of particular interest as it has known a continuous influx of migrants since the first waves of "guest workers" in the 1950s. This has led to a migrant population of 21.2 million (Statistisches Bundesamt, 2020), out of which 10.1 million are first generation, and 11.1 million second generation migrants. This significant migration inflow allows for the study of generational differences between migrants. Furthermore, being one of the most advanced economies of the European Union, Germany presents vast opportunities for highly educated migrants, on which we focus in this study. Ultimately, the diverse complexity characterizing the social and working environment in Germany has led to legislation on equal treatment (Allgemeines Gleichbehandlungsgesetz, 2006), which stipulates that discrimination based on race, ethnicity, gender, religion, age, disability, or sexual identity is strictly prohibited. Therefore, we expect this interplay between a highly international society and workplace, and anti-discrimination laws to yield interesting results.

Our interviewees have been working in a wide range of industries, professions, positions, employing organizations, career stages and were of various ethnical backgrounds and both genders. This diversity of our respondents enabled us to identify results across those criteria (Eisenhardt & Graebner, 2007; Welch, Piekkari, Plakoyiannaki & Paavilainen-Mäntymaki, 2011), thus strengthening the robustness of our conclusions. All interviews were face-to-face, except for a few interviews held via telephone or Skype. Moreover, the researchers' background is of advantage in this context. Both researchers speak German as their mother tongue, enabling them to maintain the authenticity of the respondents' perspective (Langley, 1999) and keeping the conceptual equivalence of their accounts during the data analysis (Squires, 2009).

For our specific research purposes, we had several sampling criteria. Firstly, we looked for highly qualified migrants working in Germany. We purposely selected both, first and second generation migrants (of both genders) in order to find potential differences between these two groups (see Table 1). Additionally, the interviewees worked in a broad variety of industries and functional areas to increase the robustness of our findings (see Table 2).

Table 1: Overview of the interviewees according to their generational status, gender, and ethnic countries

Generational status	Gender	Ethnic countries	Number of interviews
first generation	male	Argentina, Australia, Bolivia, China, Colombia, France, Hungary, India, Italy, Netherlands, Mexico, Pakistan, Peru, Russia, Senegal, Spain, United Kingdom, United States of America, Venezuela	24
	female	Argentina, Brazil, China, Croatia, France, India, Iran, Italy, Lithuania, Mexico, Palestine, Peru, Poland, Romania, Russia, South Africa, Spain, Taiwan, Thailand, Turkey	34
second generation	male	Bosnia, Brazil, Bulgaria, Canada, China, Croatia, France, Greece, Italy, Kazakhstan, Mexico, Palestine, Philippines, Romania, Russia, Serbia, South Africa, South Korea, Turkey, United Kingdom, United States of America, Vietnam	33
	female	Algeria, Argentina, Bosnia, Bulgaria, Canada, China, Croatia, Greece, India, Italy, Kazakhstan, Lebanon, Peru, Philippines, Poland, Romania, Russia, Serbia, Slovakia, Sri Lanka, Sweden, Turkey, United States of America, Uzbekistan, Vietnam	39

Table 2: Overview of the interviewees according to their industries and functional areas

Industry	Number of interviews	Functional area	Number of interviews
Aerospace	1	Accounting	2
Automotive manufacturer	14	Analysis	13
Automotive supplier	26	Architecture	1
Bank	7	Assistance	15
Car sharing	2	CEO	1
Construction	1	Consulting	1
Consulting	5	Controlling	2
Energy	1	Customer care/ service	8
Exhibition planning	1	Data management	1
Fashion	8	Design	1
Floriculture	1	Distribution	1
Food processing	1	Division management	2
Healthcare	4	HR	7
Hotel	1	IT	4
Household entertainment technology	1	Logistics	1
Household products	2	Management	1
Industrial and mechanical engineering	7	Marketing	3
Insurance	2	Product and business development	1
Medical services	8	Product engineering	36
Music apparel	1	Product management	1
No industry mention	3	Purchasing	8
Pharmacology	4	Quality management and sales	1
Professional training	2	Regulatory	1
Real estate	2	Research	4

Research centre	4	Research and customer care	1
Software development	11	Research and division management	1
Technology services	3	Sales	10
Textile	3	Sales and production	1
Transportation	2	Software consulting	1
Wholesale	2	Textile engineering	1

2.3.3   Data collection

We considered semi-structured and problem-centered interviews as the best means to obtain the required information for addressing our research question. On the one side, they allow in-depth learning about the perceptions of the individual interviewees by means of specific follow-up questions (Weiss, 1994), and on the other side, they allow for comparability between the interviews through asking similar key questions. Furthermore, semi-structured interviews provide the researcher with the opportunity to investigate previously unanticipated issues (Myers, 2008). For example, we initially did not expect gender-based discrimination to be such a prominent issue in this study about (ethnic-based) discrimination of migrants. However, the topic of gender discrimination at work was a recurring topic among our female interviewees. Therefore, we soon included this issue in our interview protocol, allowing for the comparison of the magnitude of gender- and ethnic-based discrimination.

The interviews consisted of open-ended questions, permitting an in-depth investigation of our respondents' perceptions and the clarification of unclear accounts (Witzel, 2000). Our interview protocol was organized according to standard procedures for semi-structured interviews (Kvale, 1996) and consisted of four sections. We started the interviews with general background information about the respondents' age, nationality, educational background, professional background, generational status in relation to the migration to Germany, years of stay and work in Germany (1st generation migrants only), reasons for migration (1st generation migrants only). The following section focused on aspects such as cultural identity or language preferences. We then moved on to questions about potential disadvantages from having a migration background in the private (i.e., non-professional) sphere. Respondents concentrated in their accounts on contexts such as own schooling experiences, search for housing, contacts with government administration and general contacts with Germans. We focused in this section on questions such as "Did you ever feel generally disadvantaged in Germany because of your migration background?", "How did you react to your teacher's treatment pertaining to your migration background?" or "How did you react to the constant house application rejections?". The last and most important part of our interview protocol focused on perceived discrimination at the workplace. Here we distinguished between discrimination in terms of recruitment, discriminatory behaviour from colleagues ,and in terms of promotion. To be more precise, we asked our interviewees questions such as "Do you feel that it took you longer to get a job than it should have?", "How do you feel that your colleagues perceive you in relation to your migration background?" and "How do you perceive your advancement opportunities at work?". Taking into consideration the sensitivity of the research topic, the migratory background of the first author, who did the largest part of the interviews, was of clear advantage. Being a highly qualified migrant in Germany herself, who has grown up with two cultures and languages, she could easily empathize with the interviewees. Thus, interviewees felt free to openly discuss the delicate issue of discrimination. To achieve investigator triangulation, 69 interviews were conducted by 13 Master students within a seminar on applied qualitative research methods. This made the comparison and contrasting of findings possible, thus decreasing potential bias in the interpretation of the results (Denzin, 2017; Yeung, 1995). In order to ensure consistency across all interviews and construct validity, the first author designed the interview guideline, tested it in her first interviews and subsequently discussed it in detail with the other interviewers (Sinkovics, Penz & Ghauri, 2008). The interviews were conducted mainly in German, as most interviewees were either already comfortable enough with the mainstream language (first generation) or had German as a mother tongue (second generation). Some interviews were held in English, Romanian, or in Spanish, in order to accommodate the language requests of the interviewees (first generation). This posed no difficulty as the first author and her Master students are highly proficient in English. Furthermore, Master students who had Spanish as mother tongue conducted some of the interviews in Spanish, at the request of some first generation interviewees.

Interviews lasted 1 hour on average with the shortest interview taking 31 minutes and the longest interview 1 hour and 33 minutes. All interviews were transcribed in their original language to maintain the contextual sense of the interviewees' statements (Bryman & Bell, 2007; Squires, 2009). All codes were labelled, however, in English and the quotations we used for illustration in this paper were translated in English if necessary. Our final data set consisted of 130 semi-structured interviews with first- and second-generation highly qualified migrants working in Germany. All interviews were taped and transcribed verbatim which resulted in 1650 pages of double-spaced data.

2.3.4   Data analysis

We followed Gioia et al. (2013) and Locke (2001) in analysing the first interviews, while still doing further interviews. For the data analysis we used the qualitative research software Atlas.ti. Some codes were taken directly from the data (for example, the quote "Finding housing was always an issue" was coded as "Difficulties finding housing"). Other codes, which marked existing theoretical concepts, were taken from the literature (for example, the quote "I received comments at work such as – the Turk -'" was labelled with the code "Ethnic ascribing at work"). Table 3 provides a more detailed overview of exemplary quotes and corresponding first order codes.

Table 3. Examples of quotes from the interviews and first order codes

Examples of interview quotations	First order concepts
Finding accomodation was problematic. (female, first generation, Peru, translated, 23022016)	Difficulties finding housing
Finding a proper accomodation is always an issue. (female, first generation, China, translated, 28092018)	
In companies I am usually seen as the Asian (female, second generation, Vietnam, translated, 13052015)	

I used to think that I was seen as an equal but when the Greek debt crisis erupted, suddenly I was only the Greek to them (male, second generation, Greece, translated, 23022016)	Ethnic ascribing at work
I have never felt like I was not part of this society. Germans are taught to accept anybody. So I did not have bad experiences. (female, first generation, Croatia, translated, 29062016)	Fair treatment from locals
I have not had bad experiences due to my cultural values or background (male, second generation, China-Vietnam, translated, 29032016)	

As a next step in our analysis, we applied the constant comparative method by regularly switching back and forth between the existing literature and our data (Glaser & Strauss, 1967; Locke, 2001). Our analysis comprised three consecutive levels of data aggregation. To generate first order codes, we applied Strauss and Corbin's (1998) method of open coding, as we remained close to our respondents' perceptions and wording choice (Gioia et al., 2013). We carefully went through each passage of our interviews and tagged each relevant statement with an appropriate first order code. In order to reduce the amount of first order codes (Gioia et al., 2013) and make more conceptual sense out of them, we then proceeded with the constant comparative method, comparing these first order codes and looking for similarities and differences between them (Strauss & Corbin, 1998). In this step of our analysis, we searched in particular for reappearing labels between generations of migrants and across job contexts. This allowed for subsequent aggregation, while ensuring that the resulting second-order codes accurately reflected our first-order codes. In this manner we moved from a primarily descriptive to a more conceptual level of codes (Van Laer & Janssens, 2011). For example, the codes "humour related to ethnic background at work from colleagues" and "feeling of exclusion at work because of being foreign" were consolidated into the second order code "microaggressions at work" (Figure 1). During this phase of coding aggregation, our analysis revealed, for example, the contrast between ethnic- and gender-based discrimination. Throughout the interviews and the coding processes we cycled back and forth within our data between different groups of interviewees and between our data and the existing literature. We compared and juxtaposed in particular statements of the first and second generation migrants in their experience of possible discrimination. During this entire process of analysis, we continuously refined the emerging core findings from our data until a saturation point was reached and no new information could be derived from the interpretation of our data (Locke, 2001).

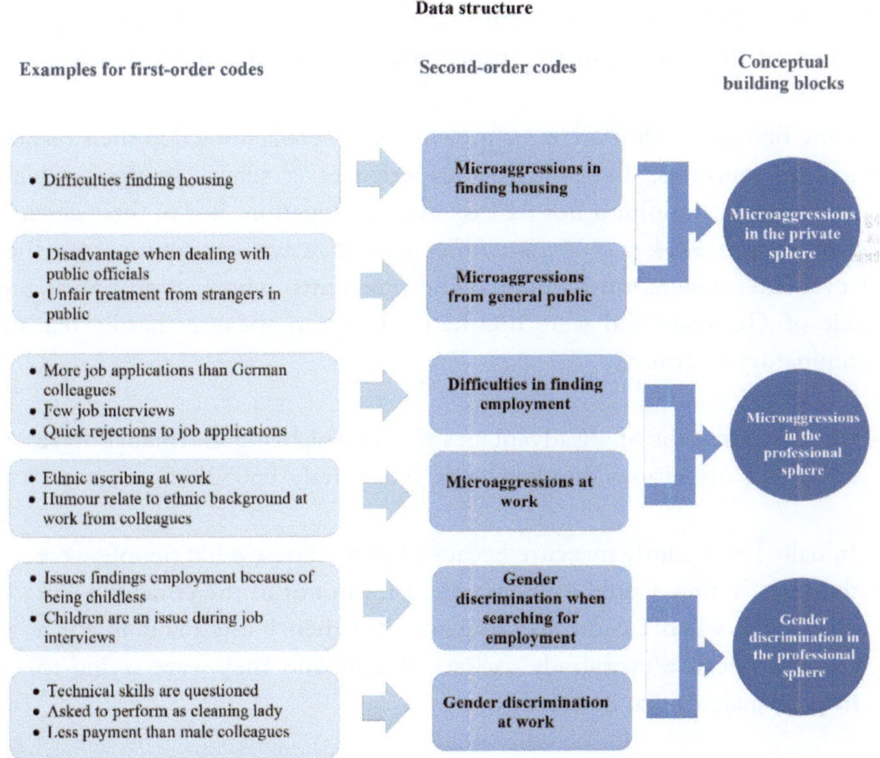

Figure 1. Examples of first order codes, second order codes, and conceptual building blocks

2.4 Findings

In the following, we will depict the perceptions of discriminatory experiences of highly qualified first generation migrants in various personal and work related domains, followed by highly qualified second generation migrants. Since not all discrimination cases are reported and oftentimes are difficult to prove, and as migrants are our only data source, we will only refer to (subjective) perceptions of migrants and not to (objective) discriminatory occurrences. We do not consider this a disadvantage of our study, to the contrary, given that this study is not about discrimination per se but about migrants' subjective experiences of discriminatory occurrences, how they react to those and what organizations and individual managers need to do in order to alleviate those experiences.

2.4.1 Perceptions of discriminatory experiences of highly qualified first generation migrants in their private sphere

Since the first generation migrants grew up and were schooled in their respective ethnic countries, discriminatory experiences at school in the receiving country were by definition not part of our investigation. But in their *unspecific social contact with members of the mainstream population*, we were quite astonished that even first generation highly qualified migrants, who had an upbringing outside of Germany and were non-native German speakers hardly felt any discriminatory treatment.

> I do not see a lot of disadvantages due to not being German. I have never had any serious disadvantages. (male, Italy, 05052016)

> Initially I was a little insecure because I didn't know what people were thinking, if they would welcome me. I mean not in the company, but in general, when I came to Germany. But then I was really in for a surprise because everybody was so friendly and they were trying to help. (female, India, 21092018)

This finding held true irrespective of demographic differentiators such as gender or age. This outcome is in contrast to previous research which found that discriminatory experiences are part of migrant's acculturation process (see, e.g. Vedder et al., 2007). This finding also contrasts with the current political situation in Germany (with the rise of an ultra right-wing and highly xenophobic political party), and the general social discourse which revolves around the "problem" of close to one million refugees who came to Germany mostly in 2015, labelled in certain contexts as "asylum tourists". We became very soon aware of this highly surprising finding emerging from our interviews and therefore, from early on, discussed such statements closer with our interviewees, also raising with them the possibility of blocking out any discriminatory experiences in order to feel more accepted in the receiving country, Germany. However, this was, after some reflection, strongly denied by our respondents. Having made the point that our interviewees do not perceive themselves as confronted with outright discrimination in unspecific social contact with members of the mainstream population, they still described various unpleasant situations. However, we note that they did not regard these as discriminatory:

> I used to live in a dorm for 2 years and one of my former roommates was German, born and raised here with barely any experience with foreigners. He hardly travelled, had little formal education and interacted only very little with others. And when I did something he did not like, he always used to say: 'You did not understand this very well, just like with the language and such'. And I would always answer: 'yeah, yeah, sure. (female, Lithuania, 05082016, TR[2])

In these cases, our first generation migrants did not necessarily feel discriminated per se but regarded these subtle and short remarks as only slightly derogatory. Our findings thus sustain current research that blatant ethnic discrimination has been substituted by more subtle and indirect forms, such as microinvalidations (Sue et al., 2009), which are sometimes meant to communicate an intellectual inferiority (Sue, Capodilupo & Holder, 2008) from the local members of the receiving society. Since our first generation interviewees did

---

[2] TR = translated

not give much value to such remarks, they also dismissed them as discriminatory behaviour which should be actively sanctioned. Accordingly, they were not overly concerned about these incidents:

> One has to learn to cope with it…in the private sphere, should there be anybody unhappy with me, I say to myself 'so what?' and search for other people I can spend my time with. (female, Lithuania, 05082016, TR)

In comparison, regarding their *contact with public officials*, first generation migrants complained significantly more about not being treated equally. In this context, one has to take into account that first generation migrants are confronted with additional bureaucracy compared to local members of the mainstream population. These bureaucratic hurdles are present in each receiving country, making it an universal migratory aspect with which one is confronted upon relocation. Nevertheless, it seems that it is not the additional bureaucratic paperwork first generation migrants have to do that is perceived as discriminatory, but it is the way they are treated by public authorities:

> One has to waste so much time and then the public officials are anything but friendly and helpful. One has the feeling that one begs for something. And even though I have a residency permit, I am very often held by officials at the airport and asked: 'What are you doing here?'. I clearly feel disadvantaged in these cases. (male, Colombia, 20042016, TR)

These discouraging interactions meant to demean and highlight a migrant's foreign status (Sue et al., 2009) are usually deeply ingrained in the behaviour of the perpetrators (Williams, 2020), and are a common occurrence. Since first generation migrants are very much made aware of their legally secondary status in the receiving country, they usually do not adventure in taking action against them.

Housing issues were equally mentioned by first generation migrants. Several of our interviewees perceived discriminatory treatment from landlords in that they had more difficulties finding an accommodation:

> Oh, it is horrible. Yes, it is really bad with the apartments. It is always a nightmare because when they see a foreign name, then that's it. Unless you actually call them and speak to them in German to convince them: 'hey, okay, I can speak your language'. That kind of helps.' (female, India, 22042016)

Since the process of tenant selection is anything but transparent, first generation migrants are put into a catch-22 like situation (Lilienfeld, 2017; Sue et al., 2009), i.e. they have difficulty in assessing the reason behind locals' decisions and behaviour, and thus do not know how to react to it. In order to probe whether the issues of finding housing arose from an unbalanced estate market or from landlords having concerns about prospective foreign tenants, some of our interviewees recurred to using two sets of applications:

> My boyfriend and I were looking for an apartment. And we tried it with the same introductory text everywhere. He is a research assistant and I work at [company name] as an engineer. And when he signed the introductory text with his German name, we would receive on the same evening an answer. And when we would sign the text with my Lithuanian name, we used to receive an answer after one or two weeks, or even no answer at all. (female, Lithuania, 05082016, TR)

Our findings concur with previous research regarding the housing discrimination of ethnic minorities, i.e. housing is refused to immigrants at the advantage of members of the mainstream population (e.g. Berry & Bell, 2012; Valentine et.al., 1999). Also, outright discrimination is relatively easy to identify. Therefore, explicit discriminatory treatment could easily be reported to authorities and is punishable on legal grounds (Van Laer & Janssens, 2011). Our findings are thus in accordance with recent discrimination literature (Deitch et.al., 2003; Basford et al., 2014; Van Laer & Janssens, 2011), that blatant discrimination is being nowadays replaced by subtle discriminatory treatment, which is harder to recognize, to report and accordingly, to penalize. Therefore, in the case of housing, first generation highly qualified migrants experienced subtle discriminatory treatment in which they were denied a fair housing application process. This all takes place without being given a transparent reason for the housing rejections, since providing the real motivation behind their turndowns would have made the landlords punishable on legal grounds. It seems that only upon resorting to specific control mechanisms such as sending fake housing applications, does the discriminatory behaviour become apparent.

Overall, it seems that in the contact with authorities and in the search for housing, first generation migrants were more prone to experience and identify microaggressions by contrast to their daily interaction with mainstream locals.

2.4.2　Perceptions of discriminatory experiences of highly qualified first generation migrants in their professional sphere

In terms of the professional sphere, we investigated discriminatory perceptions with regard to job search and general treatment at the workplace. Regarding the job search, it should be noted that all our interviewees were already employed and therefore had subsequently been successful in their job search. Nevertheless, we have had several interviewees who mentioned having had difficulties in finding employment:

> I got rejections within an hour from applying for jobs. And then you look at their requirements, then look at your own CV, and there is a match. And you have no idea why you got rejected. (female, India, 22032016)

In spite of this, it is noteworthy that few interviewees mentioned these aspects and it would not be realistic to expect an insight into the job candidates' selection processes. Since we focused on perceptions and, as mentioned above, our interviewees were all already in stable white collar positions at multinational companies, we pose that these grievances might not necessarily have an ethnic disadvantage as a source. Furthermore, the large majority of our first generation interviewee mentioned barely having dealt with discriminatory experiences upon searching for employment:

> No, so at [company name] I have never had the impression that because of nationality or something like that, it would be more difficult or different. I think that it was not so difficult for me. (male, Hungary, translated, 2502018)

> I believe that I took the normal amount of time…a friend of mine who also finished his Ph.D. and is German also needed six months. So the amount of time was normal. (male, Argentina, translated, 25062016)

> I talked to my German colleagues about it and they said they needed just as much time, if not even longer than me, to find a job. (male, Colombia, translated, 20042016)

However, it was recognized that people with a migration background in general might see themselves disadvantaged in finding a job.

> Well, I personally never felt disadvantaged when looking for a job. But I know, of course, that this is a topic for many foreigners … yes, or for many with a migration background. This is definitely an issue even though I have never experienced it personally. So I was lucky. (male, Senegal, 08052018, TR)

This generally positive evaluation contrasts starkly with previous studies (e.g., Hanewinkel, 2012; Kaas & Manger, 2011) that found that discrimination on the job market is existent, even for highly qualified migrants. Our results also contrast with previous research (Tuchik Hakak & Al Ariss, 2013) on hiring processes of migrants which found that migrants experience under- or unemployment. We explain our deviant findings with the fact that highly qualified migrants usually relocate to countries where their skills and abilities are also needed and looked for, such as in engineering (Portes & Fernandez-Kelly, 2008), or even in leadership positions (Mattoo et al., 2008). The economic situation in Germany has been over many years quite favourable, with companies having problems to fill in their positions, especially in the South, where we conducted the majority of our interviews (Bundesministerium für Wirtschaft und Energie, 2020). This speaks overall in favour of migrants with the necessary skill set. Also, the demographic situation (aging society) is an additional favouring factor for migrants with higher skills to fill in open positions (Bundesministerium für Wirtschaft und Energie, 2020).

Concerning *discriminatory treatment at the workplace*, highly qualified first generation migrants hardly reported any discriminatory treatment:

> So I never had that kind of situation were I was not comfortable, I always had that kind of good groove, here in my new job as well. (male, India, 25020216)

> I have the feeling that I am like the others, all treat me kindly, so either kind or neutral but negatively, no, I do not think so. (male, Argentina, 25062016, TR);

> I'd say I had a very, very nice workplace, good coworkers, good managers. I don't think I would have stayed or manage to stay for eight years if they weren't. (female, USA, 24030216)

Consequently, our interviewees did not feel outright discriminated due to their migration background. Having said this, respondents still reported minor and more subtle incidents at the workplace which were, however, not directly targeted at them, but at foreigners generally:

> I overheard a few times some ridiculous jokes about Russians, that they drink a lot and the like. (male, Russia, 25012016, TR)

> No, that is never the case, there is never a really mean comment. I have never heard something like 'you [Poles] are idiots'. That was never the case, but it is always a little bit pejorative, a little bit sarcastic, a little bit 'funny', this is how it is communicated. This is always a short underlying message… (female, Poland, 17062016, TR)

This finding of more subtle prejudices and negative comments about the foreign background concurs with previous research on highly qualified migrants that they are more likely to experience more subtle forms of discrimination (Hakak, Holzinger & Zikic, 2010; Sue et al., 2009). Additionally, our findings correspond well with Van Laer & Janssens (2011), especially on the idea that subtle discrimination at work is characterised by ambiguity. Thus, instead of blatant discriminatory treatment, migrants are rather confronted with microaggressions (Sue et al., 2008) in the form of subtle derogatory statements at the workplace. Since these statements are not outwardly directed at our first generation migrants but are made "on the go" and are well concealed in sarcasm or humour, first generation migrants refrain from sanctioning this type of behaviour.

Overall, first generation migrants did feel disadvantaged by having a foreign background when looking for housing or when in contact with public officials by contrast to the general interaction with locals. Nevertheless, they mostly did not perceive being disadvantaged in their professional sphere, neither when looking for employment, nor after having found employment. This positive finding contrasts starkly with previous research that found that migrants face discrimination not only when searching for employment, but also after having found one (Al Ariss, 2010; Almeida et al., 2016). However, they seem to be confronted with microaggressions at the workplace, which take a more subtle form of invalidation or othering (Friedlaender, 2018; Sue et al., 2009; Sue et al., 2008; Williams, 2020). These statements, which are skilfully veiled under humour or sarcasm, are difficult to point out and thus penalize (Friedlaender, 2018).

2.4.3 Perceptions of discriminatory experiences of highly qualified second generation migrants in their private sphere

In this second part of our findings, we report on the discriminatory perceptions of the *second generation* of highly skilled migrants, focusing again first on the private sphere and subsequently on the professional sphere. By contrast to the first generation, second generation migrants grew up and were educated in the mainstream society. Therefore, their contact with members of the mainstream population was significantly more intensive, particularly in the formative phase. This allowed us to also inquire about any discriminatory experiences at school, which was not possible for first generation migrants. By contrast, due to the fact that second generation migrants usually had the German citizenship, discriminatory experiences with government authorities played a negligible role, so that we decided not to report about them here. Another important difference was that our interviewees from the second generation are all German native speakers and did not feel any disadvantage in speaking German. Having grown up in the mainstream society, they all felt fully adapted to the local context (see also Fitzsimmons, 2013). Consequently, their behaviour and communication were entirely moulded by the mainstream society (Fitzsimmons, 2013).

Having grown up in the mainstream society, second generation migrants felt even less confronted with *discriminatory treatment by* members of the mainstream population:

> No, I was never treated differently because of my foreign origin. (male, Romania, 29062016, TR)

> No, I never perceived any disadvantages from it [having a migration background]. (female, Slovakia, 10022016, TR)

The few second generation interviewees who reported having felt treated unfavourably by members of the mainstream population were not Caucasian, i.e. their migration background was easily identifiable. But also in these cases, the form of discrimination took a subtle form:

> Well, when people see me, they begin talking differently to me…. I do not notice that I am brown, but only when I am in a room full of white people, then I notice it. (male, India-Pakistan, 17102015, TR)

Therefore, skin complexion clearly triggered a more biased behaviour from members of the mainstream population, also towards second generation migrants, who were born and raised in Germany and spoke German as their mother tongue. The form of invalidation was in all cases described as mild and subtle, often not even being meant as discriminatory. Frequently recounted occurrences usually went like this: an ethnic German upon seeing a second generation migrant with a darker skin tone asking: *"Where are you coming from?"*; second generation migrant in Swabian, the local accent: *"From Böblingen"* [small town close to Stuttgart]; ethnic German: *"I understand, but where are you* really *coming from?"*; alternatively the ethnic German replies: *"Oh, you speak very well German."*; answer from second generation migrant: *"Thank you, you too."* It thus seems that also in the case of second generation migrants, microinsults (Sue et al., 2009) were a common occurrence in the private sphere. But our second generation migrants did usually resort to microinterventions (Sue, Alsaidi, Awad, Glaeser, Calle & Mendez, 2019) in which they tried to make members of the mainstream society without a migratory background aware of their demeaning statements.

Furthermore, in longer conversations, the fact that the second generation migrants speak fluently German counterbalanced the impact of skin complexion:

> As soon as one begins talking German to the others, they do not get the feeling anymore of talking to a foreigner. (male, India-Pakistan, translated, 17102015)

So besides microinterventions (Sue et al., 2019), proficient mainstream language skills can be put to use to counteract microinsults. This way, second generation migrants seek to prove their innate mainstream societal membership.

Schooling was a context in which highly skilled second generation migrants recalled with a relatively higher degree discriminatory experiences. Even though they usually did well at elementary school, their teachers often recommended them to continue their schooling in a lower level secondary school:

> Although I had grades good enough for a higher level high school [German: Gymnasium], my teachers insisted that I should go to lower level high school [German: Realschule]. They said that because I also go to a Greek school, I would have a hard time in the Gymnasium. I would not make it there. (male, Greek, 23022016, TR)

Our findings are consistent with those of Kristen (2002) and Sprietsma (2013) who equally found that children with a migration background usually receive less recommendations for a higher quality school than children without a migration background despite having good grades, respectively have to cope with lower expectations from teachers overall. This ultimately leads to negative consequences for the future educational and career prospects of second generation migrants. Nevertheless, our interviewees managed to overcome these barriers, for example by fulfilling additional educational requirements such as attending further preparatory institutions to be able to enter tertiary educational sectors.

> It was 2003, I think, that I had finished my apprenticeship…and then
> I pursued a one-year vocational school and then I did my technical
> diploma, and afterwards it was clear that the next step would be uni-
> versity studies. (male, Turkey, 09112015, TR)

Housing, by contrast, was never mentioned by second generation migrants to
be an issue. Due to the fact that second generation migrants grew up in the
mainstream society (Crul & Doomernik, 2003; Westin, 2003; Worbs, 2003),
they are not only native speakers of the receiving country's language and fully
acculturated into its society, but also master practical aspects such as the search
for housing. This practical aspect distinguishes them from first generation migrants, who are confronted with an unknown local housing market. And, as
highly educated people with well-paying jobs, they feel no disadvantages,
which goes against prior studies. However prior studies were usually not based
on this specific subset of migrants, respectively the highly educated ones.

2.4.4 Perceptions of discriminatory experiences of highly qualified second generation migrants in their professional sphere

Regarding the professional sphere, we probed also for the second generation
the discriminatory experiences in terms of job search and general treatment
at the workplace. As to the job search, the second generation of highly qualified migrants we interviewed did not perceive being disadvantaged by their
migration background:

> My message is that I do not feel being disadvantaged because of hav-
> ing a foreign name when looking for a job. (male, Jordan, 13042018,
> TR)

Also in the subsequent job interview phase, having a migration background
was not an issue in the perception of our interviewees:

> No, having a migration background was never a topic in the job inter-
> view phase. (female, Slovakia, 1002016, TR)

This contrasts to a series of studies (e.g. Carlsson, 2010; Carlsson & Rooth, 2008; Crul & Doomernik, 2003; Derous, Nguyen & Ryan, 2009; Hanewinkel, 2012; Kaas & Manger, 2011) which found that having a migration background is detrimental when looking for employment. But yet again, the main differences of those studies and ours is that we specifically focused on highly qualified migrants, which further highlights how important it is to differentiate in studies on discrimination of migrants according to their generation and educational level. Furthermore, we investigated their perception of having experienced a biased job candidate selection and not directly reported cases of discrimination.

Apart from discussing potential discrimination at the job search stage, we also asked the second generation highly qualified migrants about the general treatment at the workplace by supervisors and colleagues. Also in this case, and even more so than first generation migrants, they did not believe to have been disadvantaged:

> My migration background was never really an issue, or a problem at work. So I have never noticed someone saying something like 'Man, he is one of those, he is not capable or does not know.' No, I never experienced something like that. (male, Romania, 29062016, TR)

> No, my migration background never mattered actually. Maybe I was also lucky with my employers. No, so I have never, at [company 1], [company 2], [company 3] or [company 4] felt anything like that, no. (male, Turkey, 09112015, TR)

Despite this adamant rejection of having ever experienced any outright discrimination, interviewees provided some noteworthy comments about their relationship with ethnic German colleagues:

> We would make small jokes and such. I have also received remarks such as 'oh, the Turk' but I took them as a joke. We also had a lot of Greeks and of course one would say 'oh, the Greek again' when the whole Greek debt crisis started. So, there were also jokes about them. But nobody took them seriously, including me. (male, Turkey, translated, 09112015)

For example, when somebody said something like 'I am moving in that neighbourhood' and then received a comment like 'Why would you move to that neighbourhood? It's full of foreigners.' Then I thought to myself 'Yeah, you idiot, why would you say something like that, what is wrong with you?'. Granted, he [his colleague] did not say it directly to me, it was a discussion between two of my colleagues who were sitting right next to me. One should take it as a joke. And the fact that I have the chance to see the others' usual behaviour without any restriction because of my background is also somewhat flattering...The fact that I am brown was mentioned in a joking way. (male, India-Pakistan, translated, 17102015)

It is noteworthy that (1) occurrences such as those cited above were clearly not described by our second generation migrant respondents as discriminatory treatment; (2) that nevertheless such occurrences were still very well remembered and recounted in detail (which one would probably not be able to do if those incidents were entirely trivial); and (3) such occurrences were very frequent. Whether one wishes to perceive such behaviour by members of the mainstream population as discrimination or not (our respondents did not), is in line with Dipboye & Halverson (2004: 132) who stated that "much of today's discrimination takes a more subtle form and has slipped out of the light into the dark side of the organization"' and with the observation by Van Laer & Janssens (2011) who assessed that such acts often take the form of jokes.

It seems that just in the case of first generation migrants, second generation highly qualified migrants experience certain forms of microaggressions in the professional sphere (e.g. derogatory humour pertaining to foreigners). Nevertheless, our second generation migrants perceived these microaggressions as generally irrelevant and dismissed them as a form of humour.

2.4.5 Perceptions of gender discrimination for highly qualified first and second generation female migrants in the professional sphere

In the previous four sections, we reported that first and second generation highly qualified migrants perceived both for the private as well as the professional sphere some form of microaggressions or discrimination in response to their ethnic background. Because of the subtle form that discrimination generally took, the degree of perceptions of ethnic discrimination was – in view of the previous literature – astonishingly low. We consider this to be a result of the insidious form of microaggressions, which makes them hard to recognize or interpret. This in turn affects how those harmed by microaggressions react to them.

While our study was meant to be on ethnic discrimination, to our surprise, our female interviewees often shifted the discussion in the context of the professional sphere to gender discrimination, an aspect which is unrelated to their ethnical background. At least at the beginning of our interviews, we did not even raise this issue, given our focus on ethnic discrimination, but often the female interviewees themselves, regardless of generational status, brought up this topic, in order to make the point that ethnic discrimination was rather minor in comparison to gender discrimination:

> Yes, I have felt treated differently. If you asked me, the difference between working in Asia, based on the fact that I have worked in Malaysia and Singapore, and here, I felt racism there, but not sexism. I feel sexism here, but not racism. (female, Malay-Chinese, 15082015)

As soon as we noticed in our explorative, inductive form of data generation, that female respondents from both generations frequently raised in the interviews the topic of gender discrimination, we started to include this aspect into our set of questions, taking advantage of the flexibility of interview-based data generation and the possibility to iterate between data generation, data analysis and literature study. Given that we did not perceive any differentiation between first and second generation highly qualified female migrants, we abandon in the following the separate presentation of findings for both sub-groups and report on the issue of gender discrimination for both sub-groups combined.

It appeared that gender was an issue for our female respondents even in their stage of job search:

> Well, my gender came up in job interviews and I personally found this somewhat brash. But ok, as a woman they want to know how many

children you have and if sometimes you show up late at work because your children are sick and so on. (female, India, 17052016, TR)

My personal disadvantage is always that I do not have children of my own and still am under 40 years old. And I switched in my resume from two adopted children [of my husband] to simply children and all of a sudden, I had more invitations to job interviews. (female, Turkey, 26092015, TR)

Our results support Bobbit-Zeher's (2011: 772) findings that for women often "issues of dependability arise particularly in cases involving pregnancy or maternity". Our interviews clearly showed that women with children are seen as less dependable at work, confirming previous findings by Ortiz & Roscigno (2009). We find that highly qualified women are sometimes even denied employment because of the common assumption that women of a certain age will desire children, making it difficult to be a dependable employee for a certain amount of time. This further sustains the findings of Gutek, Cohen & Tsui (1996) that one can be confronted with denial of employment because of one's ethnicity or gender. In our research, female migrants were denied employment on the basis of their gender. Furthermore, gender became even more of an issue for these highly qualified female migrants after having found employment. This became particularly apparent when their capabilities or their position were questioned:

And in my first years, I was doing an internship, and this really happened to me: I was asked if I were able to turn on the computer!? (female, Lithuania, 05082016, TR)

I was working on an outline and I was responsible for the technical aspects. So, there were people who called and asked for the one responsible for the technical details, and I told them that it was me. Their answer was that I was a woman, and therefore I cannot understand technical issues…Also, about 3 weeks ago I was told by my colleague that I got the position that I currently have only because I am a woman, because of the women quota. And my colleague was dead serious when he told me that. (female, France, 2202016, TR)

So yes, at work there is a limit for women. There is a limit because engines are the boys' toys and not girls' toys, that is a thing. (female, Italy-Argentina, 1802015)

Experiences such as those cited above were very frequent among our female respondents. They are also fully in line with existing research (Bobbit-Zeher's, 2011; Basford et al., 2014) that women can experience invalidations from male colleagues pertaining to their skills. What is more, not only when searching for a job and in their daily interaction with their colleagues did female highly qualified migrants feel disadvantaged, but also when it came to payment and promotions. *Payment discrimination* was an issue raised by multiple interviewees since many of our female respondents reported receiving smaller salaries than their male peers in spite of being equally qualified and fulfilling the same tasks:

I think I worked at least 15% below my market value. (female, India, 17052016, TR)

Regarding the salary I have to say yes, being a woman is a disadvantage. With salary definitely. (female, Argentina, 25052016)

Our female interviewees also reported being disadvantaged in terms of task allocation and promotions:

And the thing with the promotion, I notice for example, that the projects I could definitely do, I do not receive those…I do not want to be arrogant, but my education is better than that of some colleagues, and my experience is also better. One of my colleagues has not even studied and I have an MBA, and I still get less interesting projects than him. (female, Poland, 17062016, TR)

So here, I think the glass ceiling is there and it's very clear and it's very thick. (female, China-Philippine, 15082015)

Therefore, by contrast to research stating that nowadays more subtle forms of discrimination at the workplace is on the rise (Binggeli et.al., 2013; Cortina, 2008), for highly qualified female migrants, discriminatory treatment on the basis of their gender at the workplace took more blatant forms. The reaction most of our interviewees chose when confronted with such discriminatory treatment was to invest even more additional work to prove themselves as highly qualified.

> At the beginning, at least the first years, were without any doubt hard because I thought I needed to prove myself. (female, Lithuania, 05082016, TR)

> So I really had to demonstrate why I was in that position, what I was doing and why I was there. (female, Italy-Argentina, 18102015)

Therefore, gender discrimination proved to be for highly qualified female migrants clearly more of an impediment than discrimination due to their foreign background:

> I think that being a woman is a bigger disadvantage than being a foreigner. I received less payment because I am a woman. That really irritated me, frustrated me, and I tried to talk to my supervisor about it, but he said he could not do anything…so this was more related to gender, and not to culture' (female, India, 17052016, TR)

Our discoveries do not support the double jeopardy hypothesis by Levin, Sinclair, Veniegeas & Taylor (2002) in that ethnic minority women are supposed to be confronted with a double bias: ethnicity and gender. According to our results, ethnicity is hardly relevant in the case of highly qualified (female) migrants.

To sum it all up, gender discrimination is highly prominent in the case of highly qualified migrants, regardless of generational status. Both first and second generation female migrants reported feeling discriminated when searching for a job, in their daily interaction with their peers, in payment differences, and promotion. As such, highly qualified female migrants do not necessarily suffer from a double discrimination, contrasting the findings of Levin et.al. (2002) and Hanewinkel (2012). Instead, they are confronted with a more prominent gender discrimination (Bobbit-Zeher, 2011; Berry & Bell, 2012; Gutek et al., 1996; Iredale, 2001). As one interviewee put it: Germany has sexism, and not racism at the workplace.

2.5 Discussion

Our study lies at the intersection of two research streams – (highly skilled) *migration* and *discrimination* of (highly skilled) migrants – and, as such, contributes to both. By differentiating between discrimination perceptions of low and highly qualified migrants and focussing on the latter, by contrasting the first generation with the second generation of migrants, and by looking into both the private and professional sphere, we are able to provide in many ways a more nuanced picture compared to previous studies. In addition, our consideration of gender-based discrimination allows us to put ethnic-based discrimination into perspective. As a result, our study develops a picture which in various important ways runs counter established beliefs stemming from the previous literature.

2.5.1 Theoretical implications

Most of the previous literature on migration focused on unskilled migrants (e.g. Berry & Bell, 2012; Portes & Fernandes-Kelly, 2008; Simon & Ruhs, 2008). By contrast, our study responds to the call for more research on the discrimination experiences of *highly qualified migrants* (Al Ariss et al., 2014; Guo & Al Ariss, 2015). Based on this particular segment of migrants, our findings mainly contradict previous research, which had depicted migrants as discriminated against (Berry & Sabatier, 2010), oppressed (Essers et al., 2010), and having difficulties integrating themselves in the host country (Al Ariss et al., 2012). Nevertheless, experiencing microaggressions from the mainstream society still seems to be a common occurrence (Sue et al., 2007; Vedder et al., 2007) but the practice of these behaviours take nowadays a rather subtle form, which very often is difficult to prove, report and sanction.

We thus establish that for highly skilled migrants, at least blatant discrimination was seldomly experienced, both by the first and by the second generation. In doing so, we are not suggesting that previous research, which overwhelmingly found outright discrimination of migrants, was somehow erroneous. By contrast, we stress the importance of distinguishing between the educational and professional background of migrants, and how these successful highly educated migrants perceive and react to the subtle forms of discriminatory behaviour. This conclusion also highlights the importance of investigating highly skilled migrants who have a significantly higher social status than low skilled migrants.

Furthermore, while our interviewees mainly rejected having been exposed to discriminatory behaviour, they could recount occurrences in which their migratory background was cause for somewhat segregating or invalidating remarks by members of the mainstream culture. These statements often took the form of othering remarks (e.g. in the contact with locals without a migration background) or microaggressions (e.g. derogatory remarks at the workplace) Our respondents did not perceive them as discriminatory per se, but still saw their membership of the mainstream society being questioned. As highly qualified individuals occupying well paid, white collar positions in multinational companies, it is also possible that our interviewees resorted to repressing or dismissing certain experiences related to microaggressions and label them as unfortunate events or even humour. This justification mechanism would be in line with their educational and societal status they have managed to reach. Furthermore, their coping mechanism differed, depending on the context of these occurrences. While these discriminatory incidents were more a source of discontent in the private sphere, the microaggressions they experienced at the workplace were usually dismissed as collegial humour. This is also in line with existing findings (Sue et al., 2009) that due to the well-conceived nature of microaggressions, those harmed by such demeaning remarks have difficulties in interpreting them and subsequently choosing an appropriate reaction. Therefore, we agree with Deitch et al. (2003: 1302) who called current forms of discrimination to be "attributionally ambiguous". We prefer not to contradict our interviewees who rejected the term discrimination for themselves; instead, we prefer to speak about *microaggressions* (Lilienfeld, 2017; Sue et al., 2009).

We also do not believe to play possible discrimination per se down, as we highlighted the relevance of another form of discrimination which, according to our female respondents, matters in the professional sphere significantly more than ethnic-based discrimination: *gender-based discrimination*. Since this study was meant to be exclusively about (ethnic-based) discrimination of migrants, we initially did not consider addressing gender-based discrimination. However, as qualitative research based on semi-structured interviews allows to react to unforeseen narratives, we used this to our advantage and incorporated a comparison between ethnic- and gender-based discrimination into our further interviews. In doing so, we responded to the call for investigating the complexities of the challenges female migrants face in their receiving countries (Guo & Al Ariss, 2015). This aspect matters as women are believed to face more complex issues when immigrating than men due to gender bias and family obligations (Guo & Al Ariss, 2015). In addition, this matter has become even more relevant since the number of female highly skilled migrants to the G20 economies has been increasing over the past years (OECD, 2017). Despite its relevance, the analysis of highly qualified migrants has so far focused almost exclusively on men (Kofman & Raghuram, 2006).

The outcome of this line of questioning was very clear, as our female respondents claimed having experienced gender-based discrimination when searching for employment and even after having found one, in terms of less payment, promotion opportunities and/or demeaning remarks meant to invalidate their competencies. Consequently, highly qualified female migrants consider ethnic-based discrimination as close to negligible (as do our male respondents) and gender-based discrimination, by contrast, as much more relevant. This result contrasts the overall belief that female migrants are confronted with a double disadvantage: ethnicity and gender (Hanewinkel, 2012).

While the comparison of previous studies with our research leads us to believe that higher skills of migrants are confronted with less blunt ethnic-based discrimination, the same high skills seem not to protect female migrants from gender-based discrimination. From this we conclude that gender-based discrimination appears to take more straightforward and explicit forms than skilfully veiled microaggressions related to one's ethnicity or foreign status, at least in the professional sphere.

Next to the focus on highly skilled migrants, the main purpose of our study has been to investigate *generational differences* in the discriminatory experiences between (highly skilled) first and second generation migrants. This approach, while hardly having been pursued by the previous literature, it conceptually made sense to us: due to the fact that first generation migrants move to another country later on in life (Gong, 2007), whereas second generation migrants are born and/or raised in their parents' receiving country (Worbs, 2003), we assumed potential differing discrimination patterns, with first generation migrants complaining more often about discrimination (see also Vivero & Jenkins, 1999). However, our results clearly indicate that this is much less the case than we had expected. This is for us a surprising finding, due to the fact that not only (linguistically and culturally fully literate) second generation migrants but also the (linguistically and culturally *not* fully literate) first generation migrants did not perceive to have experienced grave discriminatory situations.

We are not arguing that there are no differences between first and second generation experiences, but they are more a question of nuance than of basics. We would hold that these nuances only became visible to us due to our highly differentiating research design. Preceding studies generally focused on overall discriminatory experiences (e.g., Van Laer & Janssens, 2011), ethnic discrimination (e.g., Guo & Al Ariss, 2015) or gender discrimination (e.g., Bobbit-Zeher, 2011), either in general or in a singular discrimination context, i.e., either the private domain (e.g., housing: Valentine et al., 1999) or the professional domain (e.g., hiring: Derous et al., 2017). By contrast, our study has looked into diverse contexts with a potential for discriminatory treatment. By differentiating between multiple life contexts in the *private and the professional sphere*, and by going from contexts with less interaction with the mainstream population to contexts of daily prolonged interaction, we have been able to provide a more comprehensive illustration of discriminatory experiences, allowing us to tease out nuances.

According to our results in the *private sphere*, the first generation of highly qualified migrants did not consider themselves being discriminated against by the mainstream population, with the exception of public officials and the landlords. They are discontent about the attitude of officials at public authorities responsible for aliens (a problem second generation migrants do not face, as they usually already possess the mainstream country's citizenship). Housing is also an issue for the first generation of highly skilled migrants, supporting Valentine et al. (1999). By contrast, highly skilled second generation migrants do not report any such problems, despite the fact that also they carry foreign names. We believe that this discrepancy results from the fact that the second generation is already fully familiar with how to address practical aspects such as housing. While first generation migrants were schooled in their home country, the question about discrimination at school does not apply to them. By contrast, our second generation respondents confirm previous findings that children of migrants are receiving recommendations for lower levels of secondary schooling and are generally confronted with lower expectations from their teachers (e.g. Fernandez-Kelly, 2008; Kristen, 2002). Based on the above results, we have been able to identify certain differences between generations of highly skilled migrants in the private sphere. These differences are usually a result of their migration status and their familiarity with the host country's system.

Also concerning the *professional context*, first and second generation migrants did not consider themselves discriminated against. Given antidiscrimination legislation, antidiscrimination policies of employers, and the general social taboo of discriminatory behaviour, blatant discrimination at the workplace appears to not be much of an issue for (highly qualified) migrants (see also Deitch et al., 2003). By contrast, (highly qualified) migrants are still confronted with microaggressions. This statement support Hakak et al.'s (2010), Binggeli et al.'s (2013) and Dipboye & Halverson's (2004) conclusions that highly qualified migrants are more prone to subtle than blatant forms of discrimination in the working context. These subtle forms can be derogatory insinuations or invalidation remarks (Sue et al., 2009) which oftentimes are challenging to prove as discrimination per se.

Interestingly, the second generation is more vocal in reporting microaggressions from work colleagues. This might be the result of first generation migrants having, despite their overall fluency in the mainstream language, sometimes difficulties in comprehending certain mainstream conversations, in particular if slang is involved. As such they might miss out on some ironic remarks that are uttered at their expense. This is not a problem second generation migrants face since they are fully versed in the mainstream language, and values and norms of the mainstream society (Fitzsimmons, 2013). Hence, generational status might play a role in the ability of detecting microaggressions. By contrast, where generational status appears not to play a role is gender discrimination, as highly qualified female migrants of both first and second generation equally complain of being treated unfairly on the basis of their gender.

2.5.2 Managerial implications

The fact that highly skilled migrants of the first and second generation rejected the notion of being discriminated at the workplace are an indicator that outright (ethnic-based) discrimination has no place in (in our case: German) companies. However, this should not entice companies to become complacent in the fight of discrimination. As we have established, first and in particular second generation migrants, still see themselves at the workplace commonly confronted with microaggressions, such as othering statements, skilfully disguised as humorous remarks. Particularly for countries with declining populations, such as Germany, being able to attract highly qualified migrants and to fully integrate them into the mainstream society is of critical relevance. On the organizational level, managers should therefore foster an organizational culture that discourages any kind of segregating behaviour in the form of microinvalidations or microinsults, and creates a psychologically safe environment for every member of an increasingly diverse workforce. Monitoring and carefully dealing with situations in which migrants are confronted with microaggressions at the workplace can be an additional step managers should take.

Regarding highly qualified female migrants, we found that gender-based discrimination is still an issue in companies (see also Basford et al., 2014; Bobbit-Zeher, 2011;) and this although gender equality is very much on the agenda of governments, employing corporations and societies. Highly qualified female migrants reported about feeling disadvantaged not only regarding employment search (Ortiz & Roscigno, 2009), but also regarding payment and promotion. Implementing a solely competence- and qualification-based HRM system should continue to be a high priority topic. Managers should also facilitate a working environment in which gender discrimination is not tolerated.

Furthermore, as one interviewee recollected, the current mandatory women quota legislation seems to have had adverse effects on how female employees are perceived by their male counterparts. As a result, women's competencies and held positions are invalidated. Legislators could take these adverse effects into consideration and draft more gender-neutral legislations: mandatory implementation of gender anonymous job application platforms and/or wider child-care systems, even in partnership with employers.

2.5.3　Limitations and suggestions for future research

In terms of limitations of our study, the following aspects should be mentioned: While we covered in our interviews with highly qualified migrants a wide array of companies and industries, we kept the country of analysis, Germany, constant. In our view, this fully made sense, as we wished to exclude cultural, institutional, and economic differences between receiving countries. But we acknowledge of course that other countries might provide varying contexts that could influence discriminatory experiences in different ways.

Within Germany, we also performed most of the interviews in an economically highly prosperous region, i.e. the Southern part of Germany, which is also characterised by a low unemployment rate and a shortage of skilled labour. This might also have influenced the low degree of discrimination that we found. Had the interviews been conducted in Eastern Germany (the former GDR), where also xenophobia is more prevalent, results might have been somewhat different.[3] However, particularly highly skilled people migrate to regions where job shortages prevail (Iredale, 2001) and in this sense, our focus on an economically successful region makes fully sense.

Furthermore, we did not explore the potential differences the organizational or professional culture might play (Derous et al., 2017). As such, we encourage future studies to take these factors into consideration when examining discriminatory treatment at the workplace. Taking into account that the organizational or professional culture is especially important in the case of gender discrimination (e.g. women working in a technical, male dominated domain) as the gender configuration at the workplace might play a role in experiencing discrimination (Bobbit-Zeher, 2011).

Finally, while we focused in our study on generational differences, we also did not investigate differences in ethnicity. However, we are aware of the fact that discrimination does not impact all migrants alike (Turchick Hakak & Al Ariss, 2013). As such, we encourage future studies to also consider ethnical differences when investigating the perceptions of discriminatory experiences of highly qualified migrants.

---

[3] The obvious solution to resolve this speculation would have been to also do interviews with highly skilled migrants in Eastern Germany. However, the paradoxical problem is that while many Eastern Germans feel "overrun" by foreigners, taking "their jobs and housing away", at the same time, only few (in particular highly skilled) foreigners actually live in the Eastern states of Germany. In the city of Dresden regular demonstrations against the "Islamization of the Occident" take place, while Dresden has a Muslim population of 0.2 percent (en.wikipedia.org/wiki/Dresden).

2.5.4 Conclusion

Our study responds to the frequent calls of investigating discriminatory experiences of highly qualified migrants and, as such, advances our understanding in migration and discrimination research. Based on rich qualitative interview data, we find that for highly skilled migrants of both the first and second generation, blatant discrimination is not much of an issue, neither in the private nor the professional sphere. This important finding, which stands in stark contrast to previous studies and widely held beliefs, suggests strongly differing discrimination experiences of highly from low skilled migrants. Nevertheless, in the professional domain, in particular high qualified migrants of the second generation see themselves confronted with microaggressions. This is a problem organizations need to address. Furthermore, while ethnic-based discrimination is largely negated, highly qualified female migrants report having experienced more blunt forms of gender-based discrimination. Our study clearly shows how important it is to differentiate in migration and discrimination studies according to important factors such as educational level, generational status, private and professional context, and gender. In doing so, our study offers new paths for more nuanced investigations lying at the intersection of migration and discrimination research.

2.6 Bibliography

Al Ariss, A. (2010). Modes of engagement: migration, self-initiated expatriation, and career development. *Career Development International, 15*(4), 338-358.

Al Ariss, A., & Crowley-Henry, M. (2013). Self-initiated expatriation and migration in the management literature: Present theorizations and future research directions. *Career Development International, 18*(1), 78-96.

Al Ariss, A., Cascio, W. F., & Paauwe, J. (2014). Talent management: Current theories and future research directions. *Journal of World Business, 49*(2), 173-179.

Al Ariss, A., Koall, I., Özbilgin, M., & Suutari, V. (2012). Careers of skilled migrants: towards a theoretical and methodological expansion. *Journal of Management Development, 31*(2), 92-101.

Al Ariss, A., Vassilopoulou, J., Özbilgin, M. F., & Game, A. (2013). Understanding career experiences of skilled minority ethnic workers in France and Germany. *The International Journal of Human Resource Management, 24*(6), 1236-1256.

Allgemeines Gleichbehandlungsgesetz. (2006). Available online: https://www.antidiskriminierungsstelle.de/SharedDocs/Downloads/DE/publikationen/AGG/agg_gleichbehandlungsgesetz.pdf?__blob=publicationFile. [Accessed on 22 April 2021]

Almeida, J., Biello, K. B., Pedraza, F., Wintner, S., & Viruell-Fuentes, E. (2016). The association between anti-immigrant policies and perceived discrimination among Latinos in the US: A multilevel analysis. *SSM-Population Health, 2*, 897-903.

Bakker, W., Van Der Zee, K., & Van Oudenhoven, J. P. (2006). Personality and Dutch emigrants' reactions to acculturation strategies. *Journal of Applied Social Psychology, 36*(12), 2864-2891.

Basford, T. E., Offermann, L. R., & Behrend, T. S. (2014). Do you see what I see? Perceptions of gender microaggressions in the workplace. *Psychology of Women Quarterly, 38*(3), 340-349.

Beiser, M., Barwick, C., Berry, J.W., da Costa, G., Fantino, A., Ganesan, S., Lee, C., Milne, W., Naidoo, J., Prince, R., Tousignant, M. and Vela, E. (1988).

Mental health issues affecting immigrants and refugees. Ottawa: Health and Welfare Canada

Benet-Martínez, V., & Haritatos, J. (2005). Bicultural identity integration (BII): Components and psychosocial antecedents. *Journal of Personality, 73*(4), 1015-1050.

Berg, M. L., & Eckstein, S. E. (2009). *Re-imagining diasporas and generations*. University of Toronto Press.

Berry, D. P., & Bell, M. P. (2012). 'Expatriates': gender, race and class distinctions in international management. *Gender, Work & Organization, 19*(1), 10-28.

Berry, J. W. (1997). Immigration, acculturation, and adaptation. *Applied Psychology, 46*(1), 5-34.

Berry, J. W., & Sabatier, C. (2010). Acculturation, discrimination, and adaptation among second generation immigrant youth in Montreal and Paris. *International Journal of Intercultural Relations, 34*(3), 191-207.

Bertrand, M., & Mullainathan, S. (2004). Are Emily and Greg more employable than Lakisha and Jamal? A field experiment on labor market discrimination. *American Economic Review, 94*(4), 991-1013.

Binggeli, S., Dietz, J., & Krings, F. (2013). Immigrants: A forgotten minority. *Industrial and Organizational Psychology, 6*(1), 107-113.

Birkinshaw, J., Brannen, M. Y., & Tung, R. L. (2011). From a distance and generalizable to up close and grounded: Reclaiming a place for qualitative methods in international business research. *Journal of International Business Studies, 42*(5), 573-581.

Bobbit-Zeher, D. (2011). Institutional policies, and gender composition of workplace gender discrimination at work: Connecting gender stereotypes. *Gender & Society, 25*, 764-786.

Bovenkerk, E, M. J. I. Gras and D. Ramsoedh (1994) *Discrimination against Migrant Workers and Ethnic Minorities in Access to Employment in the Netherlands*. Geneva: ILO.

Bryman, A., & Bell, E. (2007). *Business research methods*. (2nd ed). Oxford: Oxford University Press.

Bundesministerium für Wirtschaft und Energie. (2020). Möglichkeiten der Fachkräfteeinwanderung. Was Arbeitgeber wissen müssen. Available online: https://www.bmwi.de/Redaktion/DE/Publikationen/Ausbildung-

und-Beruf/moeglichkeiten-der-fachkraefteeinwande-rung.pdf?__blob=publicationFile&v=10. [Accessed 12 February 2021]

Bundeszentrale für politische Bildung (2016). Retrieved from: http://www.bpb.de [Accessed 10 October, 2018]

Carlsson, M. (2010). Experimental Evidence of Discrimination in the Hiring of First-and Second-generation Immigrants. *Labour, 24*(3), 263-278.

Carlsson, M., & Rooth, D. O. (2007). Evidence of ethnic discrimination in the Swedish labor market using experimental data. *Labour Economics, 14*(4), 716-729.

Carlsson, M., & Rooth, D. O. (2008). Is it your foreign name or foreign quali-fications? An experimental study of ethnic discrimination in hiring. IZA discussion papers, No. 3810, Institute for the Study of Labor (IZA), Bonn. Available online: http://nbn-resolving.de/urn:nbn:de:101:1-20081126850 [Accessed on 30 September 2018]

Castles, S., De Haas, H., & Miller, M. J. (2013). *The age of migration: International population movements in the modern world.* London: Macmillan International Higher Education.

Cerdin, J. L., & Selmer, J. (2014). Who is a self-initiated expatriate? Towards conceptual clarity of a common notion. *The International Journal of Human Resource Management, 25*(9), 1281-1301.

Cerdin, J. L., Diné, M. A., & Brewster, C. (2014). Qualified immigrants' suc-cess: Exploring the motivation to migrate and to integrate. *Journal of Inter-national Business Studies, 45*(2), 151-168.

Cortina, L. M. (2008). Unseen injustice: Incivility as modern discrimination in organizations. *Academy of Management Review, 33*(1), 55-75.

Crul, M., & Doomernik, J. (2003). The Turkish and Moroccan Second Gener-ation in the Netherlands: Divergent Trends between and Polarization within the Two Groups. *International Migration Review, 37*(4), 1039-1064.

Crul, M., & Vermeulen, H. (2003). The second generation in Europe. *Interna-tional Migration Review, 37*(4), 965-986.

D'Amico, T. F. (1987). The conceit of labor market discrimination. *The Amer-ican Economic Review, 77*(2), 310-315.

Deitch, E. A., Barsky, A., Butz, R. M., Chan, S., Brief, A. P., & Bradley, J. C. (2003). Subtle yet significant: The existence and impact of everyday racial discrimination in the workplace. *Human Relations, 56*(11), 1299-1324.

Denzin, N. K. (2017). *The research act: A theoretical introduction to sociological methods*. New York: Routledge.

Derous, E., Nguyen, H. H., & Ryan, A. M. (2009). Hiring discrimination against Arab minorities: Interactions between prejudice and job characteristics. *Human Performance, 22*(4), 297-320.

Derous, E., Pepermans, R., & Ryan, A. M. (2017). Ethnic discrimination during résumé screening: Interactive effects of applicants' ethnic salience with job context. *Human Relations, 70*(7), 860-882.

Diehl, C., & Koenig, M. (2009). Religiosität türkischer Migranten im Generationenverlauf: Ein Befund und einige Erklärungsversuche/Religiosity of First and Second Generation Turkish Migrants: A Phenomenon and Some Attempts at a Theoretical Explanation. *Zeitschrift für Soziologie, 38*(4), 300-319.

Dipboye, R. L., & Colella, A. (2005). The dilemmas of workplace discrimination. In Dipboye, R. L., & Colella, A. (Eds) *Discrimination at work: The psychological and organizational bases* (pp. 425-462). New York: Psychology Press

Dipboye, R. L., & Halverson, S. K. (2004). Subtle (and not so subtle) discrimination in organizations. In Griffin, R., W., O'Leary-Kenny, A., M., (Eds) *The dark side of organizational behaviour* (pp 131-158). San Francisco: John Wiley and Sons.

Edmondson, A. C., & McManus, S. E. (2007). Methodological fit in management field research. *Academy of Management Review, 32*(4), 1246-1264.

Eisenhardt, K. M., & Graebner, M. E. (2007). Theory building from cases: Opportunities and challenges. *The Academy of Management Journal, 50*(1), 25-32.

Essers, C., Benschop, Y., & Doorewaard, H. (2010). Female ethnicity: Understanding Muslim immigrant businesswomen in the Netherlands. *Gender, Work & Organization, 17*(3), 320-339.

European Commission against racism and intolerance (2017). *Annual report on ECRI's activities*. Available online: https://rm.coe.int/annual-report-on-ecri-s-activities-covering-the-period-from-1-january-/16808c168b [Accessed on 15 August 2018]

Fernández-Kelly, P. (2008). The back pocket map: Social class and cultural capital as transferable assets in the advancement of second-generation immigrants. *The ANNALS of the American Academy of Political and Social Science, 620*(1), 116-137.

Fitzsimmons, S. R. (2013). Multicultural employees: A framework for understanding how they contribute to organizations. *Academy of Management Review*, *38*(4), 525-549.

Friedlaender, C. (2018). On microaggressions: Cumulative harm and individual responsibility. *Hypatia*, *33*(1), 5-21.

Gioia, D. A., Corley, K. G., & Hamilton, A. L. (2013). Seeking qualitative rigor in inductive research: Notes on the Gioia methodology. *Organizational Research Methods*, *16*(1), 15-31.

Glaser, B. G., & Strauss, A. L. (1967). *Discovery of grounded theory: Strategies for qualitative research*. New York: Routledge.

Gong, L. (2007). Ethnic identity and identification with the majority group: Relations with national identity and self-esteem. *International Journal of Intercultural Relations*, *31*(4), 503-523.

Guo, C., & Al Ariss, A. (2015). Human resource management of international migrants: current theories and future research. *International Journal of Human Resource Management*, *26*(10), 1287-1297.

Gutek, B. A., Cohen, A. G., & Tsui, A. (1996). Reactions to perceived sex discrimination. *Human Relations*, *49*(6), 791-813.

Hajro, A., Zilinskaite, M., & Stahl, G. (2017). Acculturation of Hhighly-qualified Migrants: Individual Coping Strategies and Climate for Inclusion. In *Academy of Management Proceedings* (Vol. 2017, No. 1, p. 13666). Briarcliff Manor, NY 10510: Academy of Management.

Hakak, L. T., Holzinger, I., & Zikic, J. (2010). Barriers and paths to success Latin American MBAs' views of employment in Canada. *Journal of Managerial Psychology*, 25(2), 159–176

Hamilton, J. A., Alagna, S. W., King, L. S., & Lloyd, C. (1987). The emotional consequences of gender-based abuse in the workplace: New counseling programs for sex discrimination. *Women & Therapy*, *6*(1-2), 155-182.

Hanewinkel, V. (2012). *Kurzdossier, Focus MIGRATION, Aus der Heimat in die Heimat, Die Abwanderung hochqualifizierter türkeistämmiger deutscher Staatsangehöriger in die Türkei*. Herausgeber: IMIS der Universität Osnabrück.

Heath, A. F., Rothon, C., & Kilpi, E. (2008). The second generation in Western Europe: Education, unemployment, and occupational attainment. *Annual Review of Sociology*, *34*, 211-235.

Iredale, R. (2001). The migration of professionals: theories and typologies. *International Migration*, *39*(5), 7-26.

Kaas, L., & Manger, C. (2011). Ethnic discrimination in Germany's labour market: a field experiment. *German Economic Review, 13*(1), 1-20.

Kofman, E., & Raghuram, P. (2006). Gender and global labour migrations: Incorporating skilled workers. *Antipode, 38*(2), 282-303.

Kristen, C. (2002). Hauptschule, Realschule oder Gymnasium?. *KZfSS Kölner Zeitschrift für Soziologie und Sozialpsychologie, 54*(3), 534-552.

Kvale S (1996) *InterViews. An Introduction to Qualitative Research Interviewing.* Thousand Oaks, CA: SAGE.

Langley, A. (1999). Strategies for theorizing from process data. *Academy of Management Review, 24*(4), 691-710.

Laurent, A. (1986). The cross-cultural puzzle of international human resource management. *Human Resource Management, 25*(1), 91-102.

Levin, S., Sinclair, S., Veniegeas, R., C., Taylor, P., L. (2002). Perceived discrimination in the context of multiple group memberships. *American Psychological Society,* 13(6), 557-560

Lilienfeld, S. O. (2017). Microaggressions: Strong claims, inadequate evidence. *Perspectives on Psychological Science,* 12(1), 138-169.

Locke, K. (2001). *Grounded theory in management research.* Thousand Oaks, CA: Sage Publications.

Martin, P. (2008). Managing Mexico-US Migration: Economic and Labor Issues. In Escobar Latapi A., Martin S.F. (Eds). *Mexico-US migration management* (pp 61-88). Plymouth: Lexington Books.

Massey, D. S., & Lundy, G. (2001). Use of black English and racial discrimination in urban housing markets: New methods and findings. *Urban Affairs Review, 36*(4), 452-469.

Mattoo, A., Neagu, I. C., & Ozden, C. (2008). Brain waste? Educated immigrants in the US labor market. *Journal of Development Economics,* 87, 255-269.

McTernan, E. (2018). Microaggressions, equality, and social practices. *Journal of Political Philosophy, 26*(3), 261-281.

Myers, M. D. (2008). *Qualitative research in business and management.* Thousand Oaks, CA: Sage.

OECD (2017). G20 global displacement and migration report trends report. Available online: https://www.oecd.org/g20/topics/employment-and-social-policy/G20-OECD-migration.pdf [Accessed on 15 October 2018]

Ortiz, S. Y., & Roscigno, V. J. (2009). Discrimination, women, and work: Processes and variations by race and class. The Sociological Quarterly, 50(2), 336-359.

Pager, D., & Western, B. (2012). Identifying discrimination at work: The use of field experiments. Journal of Social Issues, 68(2), 221-237.

Pierce, C. (1970). Offensive mechanisms. In F. Barbour (Ed.), The black seventies (pp. 265-282). Boston, MA: Porter Sargent

Polek, E., van Oudenhoven, J. P., & ten Berge, J. M. (2008). Attachment styles and demographic factors as predictors of sociocultural and psychological adjustment of Eastern European immigrants in the Netherlands. International Journal of Psychology, 43(5), 919-928.

Portes, A., & Fernández-Kelly, P. (2008). No margin for error: Educational and occupational achievement among disadvantaged children of immigrants. *The Annals of the American Academy of Political and Social Science, 620*(1), 12-36.

Pratt, M. G. (2009). From the editors. For the lack of a boilerplate: tips on writing up (and reviewing) qualitative research. *Academy of Management Journal*, 52(5), 856–862.

Recchi, E., & Nebe, T. M. (2003). Migration and political identity in the European Union: Research issues and theoretical premises. *State of the Art Report, Pioneur Working Paper*, (1).

Rumbaut, R. G. (2004). Ages, life stages, and generational cohorts: decomposing the immigrant first and second generations in the United States. *International Migration Review, 38*(3), 1160-1205.

Schewel, K. (2020). Understanding immobility: Moving beyond the mobility bias in migration studies. *International Migration Review, 54*(2), 328-355.

Searle, W., & Ward, C. (1990). The prediction of psychological and sociocultural adjustment during cross-cultural transitions. *International Journal of Intercultural Relations, 14*(4), 449-464.

Silberman, R., Alba, R., & Fournier, I. (2007). Segmented assimilation in France? Discrimination in the labour market against the second generation. *Ethnic and Racial Studies, 30*(1), 1-27.

Simon, B., & Ruhs, D. (2008). Identity and politicization among Turkish migrants in Germany: the role of dual identification. *Journal of Personality and Social Psychology, 95*(6), 1354.

Sinkovics, R. R., Penz, E., & Ghauri, P. N. (2008). Enhancing the trustworthiness of qualitative research in international business. *Management International Review, 48*(6), 689-714.

Sprietsma, M. (2013). Discrimination in grading: Experimental evidence from primary school teachers. *Empirical economics, 45*(1), 523-538.

Squires, A. (2009). Methodological challenges in cross-language qualitative research: a research review. *International Journal of Nursing Studies, 46*(2), 277-287.

Statistisches Bundesamt – Destatis. (2020). *Migration und Integration.* Available online: https://www.destatis.de/DE/Themen/Gesellschaft-Umwelt/Bevoelkerung/Migration-Integration/_inhalt.html. [Accessed 22 April 2021]

Strauss, A., & Corbin, J. (1998). Basics of qualitative research: Techniques and procedures for developing grounded theory, 2nd ed. Thousand Oaks: Sage.

Sue, D. W., Alsaidi, S., Awad, M. N., Glaeser, E., Calle, C. Z., & Mendez, N. (2019). Disarming racial microaggressions: Microintervention strategies for targets, White allies, and bystanders. *American Psychologist, 74*(1), 128.

Sue, D.W., Bucceri, J.M., Lin, A.I., Nadal, K.L., & Torino, G.C. (2009). Racial microaggressions and the Asian American experience. *Asian American Journal of Psychology* S (1): 88– 101.

Sue, D. W., Capodilupo, C. M., & Holder, A. (2008). Racial microaggressions in the life experience of Black Americans. *Professional Psychology: Research and Practice, 39*(3), 329.

Sue, D. W., Capodilupo, C. M., Torino, G. C., Bucceri, J. M., Holder, A., Nadal, K. L., & Esquilin, M. (2007). Racial microaggressions in everyday life: implications for clinical practice. *American Psychologist, 62*(4), 271.

Tharenou, P. (2010). Women's self-initiated expatriation as a career option and its ethical issues. *Journal of Business Ethics, 95*(1), 73-88.

Tharenou, P. (2015). Researching expatriate types: the quest for rigorous methodological approaches. *Human Resource Management Journal, 25*(2), 149-165.

Thomson, M., & Crul, M. (2007). The second generation in Europe and the United States: How is the transatlantic debate relevant for further research on the European second generation? *Journal of Ethnic and Migration Studies, 33*(7), 1025-1041.

Turchick Hakak, L., & Al Ariss, A. (2013). Vulnerable work and international migrants: A relational human resource management perspective. *The International Journal of Human Resource Management, 24*(22), 4116-4131.

United Nations, Department of Economic and Social Affairs, Population Division (2020). *International Migration Report 2020* (ST/ESA/SER.A/403). Available online: https://www.un.org/sites/un2.un.org/files/wmr_2020.pdf [Accessed on 22 April 2021]

Valentine, S., Silver, L., & Twigg, N. (1999). Locus of control, job satisfaction, and job complexity: The role of perceived race discrimination. *Psychological Reports, 84*(3), 1267-1273.

Van Laer, K., & Janssens, M. (2011). Ethnic minority professionals' experiences with subtle discrimination in the workplace. *Human Relations, 64*(9), 1203-1227.

Van Oudenhoven, J. P., Ward, C., & Masgoret, A. M. (2006). Patterns of relations between immigrants and host societies. *International Journal of Intercultural Relations, 30*(6), 637-651.

Vedder, P., Sam, D. L., & Liebkind, K. (2007). The acculturation and adaptation of Turkish adolescents in North-Western Europe. *Applied Development Science, 11*(3), 126-136.

Vivero, V. N., & Jenkins, S. R. (1999). Existential hazards of the multicultural individual: Defining and understanding" cultural homelessness.". *Cultural Diversity and Ethnic Minority Psychology, 5*(1), 6.

Weiss, R. S. (1994). *Learning from strangers.* New York. Free Press

Welch, C., Piekkari, R., Plakoyiannaki, E., & Paavilainen-Mäntymäki, E. (2011). Theorising from case studies: Towards a pluralist future for international business research. *Journal of International Business Studies, 42*(5), 740-762.

Westin, C. (2003). Young people of migrant origin in Sweden. *International Migration Review, 37*(4), 987-1010.

Williams, M. T. (2020). Microaggressions: Clarification, evidence, and impact. *Perspectives on Psychological Science, 15*(1), 3-26.

Witzel, A. (2000). The problem-centered interview. Forum: Qualitative Social Research, 1(1), Available online: http://www.qualitative-research.net/index.php/fqs/article/view/1132/2521, accessed 15 September 2018.

Worbs, S. (2003). The second generation in Germany: between school and labor market. *International Migration Review, 37*(4), 1011-1038.

Yağmur, K., & van de Vijver, F. J. (2012). Acculturation and language orientations of Turkish immigrants in Australia, France, Germany, and the Netherlands. *Journal of Cross-Cultural Psychology, 43*(7), 1110-1130.

Yeung, H. W. C. (1995). Qualitative personal interviews in international business research: some lessons from a study of Hong Kong transnational corporations. *International Business Review, 4*(3), 313-339.

Young, H. R., Shoss, M. K., Farmer, B., & Harris, E. (2017). Formative and Reflective Conceptualizations of Broad Discrimination. In *Academy of Management Proceedings* (Vol. 2017, No. 1, p. 14369). Briarcliff Manor, NY 10510: Academy of Management.

3. Highly qualified first and second generation migrants:

how they apply their culture- and language-specific and -general skills[4]

Abstract

Based on 130 semi-structured interviews with highly qualified migrants, our inductive and explorative study investigates whether first and second generation migrants differ in the application of their cultural and language skills in multinational work contexts. We establish that first and second generation migrants possess culture- and language-*specific* skills, related to their ethnic country, which they employ to improve cross-national work relations. However, while first generation migrants have a solid knowledge of their ethnic culture and language, they still are less effective in augmenting cross-national work relations, due to their limited knowledge of the mainstream culture and language. Even more striking are differences regarding culture- and language-*general* skills: first generation migrants seem to acquire these only gradually over time, while for second generation migrants, they are an ingrained part of their skills. Our study thus clearly indicates the necessity to differentiate between generations when evaluating the cultural and language skills of highly qualified migrants.

---

[4] An earlier version of the article was accepted and presented at the European International Business Academy Meeting 2020 and at the Yearly Conference of International Management of the German Academic Association of Business Research 2020

3.1 Introduction

Multinational companies (MNCs) inherently have a cultural and linguistic diversity which stems from their international operations. Although this diversity can bring with itself certain benefits such as creativity (Hofhuis, van der Zee & Otten, 2012), it can also create challenges such as cross-cultural misunderstandings and miscommunication (Milliken & Martins, 1996). One potential solution to counteract the operational issues stemming from cultural and linguistic diversity would be to employ multiculturals (Brannen & Thomas, 2010).

Multiculturals have been defined as those individuals who comfortably understand and use their cultural repertoires, and identify with their integrated cultures (Brannen & Thomas, 2010). Although there are multiple ways through which individuals develop multicultural skills, our study focuses on migration, more specifically on migrants as a category of multiculturals (Fitzsimmons, 2013; Martin & Shao, 2016).

Given that about one in four migrants moving into the G20 economies holds at least a tertiary education degree (OECD, 2017), and that most of the migration research has focused on low skilled migrants (Kofman & Raghuram, 2006), we find this category of qualified mobile workforce to deserve a more focused attention. Initial prior research already suggested that higher educational levels could be associated with lower adaptation stress (Berry, 1997) and with a higher degree of identification with the receiving country (Polek, van Oudenhoven & ten Berge, 2008). Therefore, we find that it conceptually makes sense to differentiate between the educational levels of migrants. The present study therefore focuses on the sub-group of highly skilled migrants as an example of multiculturals.

When it comes to the integration processes of migrants into the receiving society, we argue that a generational distinction should be an imperative. First generation migrants, who can be defined as those migrants who were born in a different country from the receiving one (Gong, 2007), are confronted with both a new culture to which they need to adapt, and (frequently) with an unknown language they need to learn. By contrast, second generation migrants, who were born in the receiving country but have at least one parent from the first generation of migrants (Worbs, 2003), grow up in a multicultural environment and are therefore immersed in both cultures and languages from early on. Martin & Shao (2016) mention that first generation migrants might be able to develop an achieved multiculturalism, whereas second generation migrants enjoy an innate multiculturalism. In our literature review, we also found that many of the skills multicultural individuals are believed to hold were thought of being useful in a culture specific and language specific context. We intend to move beyond the culture specific and language specific skills, and additionally look into the culture general (Stadler, 2017) and language general skills (Cohen, Kassis-Henderson & Lecomte, 2015). These comprehensive skills which could be appliable in any given cultural context are believed to be difficult to define and investigate (Stadler, 2017).

Based on these considerations, we intend to address the following research question: *how do first and second generation highly skilled migrants differ in their multicultural and multilingual skills which they apply in an international work context?*

Through a systematic qualitative analysis of 130 semi-structured interviews with first and second generation highly skilled migrants, this study provides a more thorough picture and in-depth understanding of their multicultural and multilingual skills and how these skills are being used in an international working context. Our study thus advances research on (highly skilled) migrants and their multicultural and multilingual skills by revealing how educational and generational status have an impact in the use and development of such skills.

3.2 Literature Review

3.2.1 Multiculturals and multilinguals

The cultural and linguistic diversity that characterize multinational companies can be viewed as a "double edged sword" (Hofhuis et al., 2012: 965). On the one side, diversity can lead to higher creativity, multiple perspectives, or increased flexibility (Amaram, 2007; Hofhuis et al., 2012). On the other side, it can also contribute to misunderstandings, miscommunication (Hong, 2010), conflicts (Mazur, 2010), or even discrimination (Milliken & Martins, 1996; Pelled, Eisenhardt & Xin, 1999). As such, diversity could also be understood as a cluster of boundaries instead of resources (Carlile, 2004). For example, cultural clashes at the workplace are usually concluded in favour of the majority group, leading to the creation of communication and participation barriers between different cultural groups (Amaram, 2007). Language differences can lead to confusion due to different communication patterns (Hong & Doz, 2013) or even limited interactions between organizational members (Kostova & Roth, 2003). Deriving from these cultural and linguistic boundaries, particular challenges arise for organizational processes such as knowledge sharing (Barner-Rasmussen, Ehrnrooth, Koveshnikov & Mäkelä, 2008) or managing relations between headquarters (HQ) and foreign subsidiaries (Blazejewski & Becker-Ritterspach, 2011). As a result, cultural and linguistic diversity can negatively impact multiple organizational processes, both internally and externally (Hutzschenreuter & Voll, 2008).

MNCs must therefore find solutions pertaining to these diversity-related problems to reduce the negative effects and promote positive outcomes (Hofhuis et al., 2012). One possible solution would be to employ multicultural and multilingual individuals (Furusawa & Brewster, 2015; Hong, 2010) as their skills could potentially address some of these operational conundrums. Multiculturals and multilinguals could prove to be of organizational use when solving cross-cultural disputes (Friedman & Liu, 2009), or assisting with knowledge sharing, thus rendering them particularly valuable as strategic human capital resources (Hong & Minbaeva, 2017).

Multiculturals can be regarded as individuals who "comfortably understand and use the norms, ways of thinking and attitudes common within two cultural systems" (Friedman & Liu, 2009: 333) and who identify with their respective internalized cultures (Brannen & Thomas, 2010; Fitzsimmons, 2013; Friedman & Liu, 2009). They are believed to present certain unique characteristics such as greater empathy (Brannen, Garcia & Thomas, 2009), mental flexibility (Chiu & Hong, 2005), adaptability (Nguyen & Benet-Martinez, 2013), or cognitive complexity (Benet-Martinez, Lee & Leu, 2006). These attributes allow them to cognitively and behaviourally interpret better differing cultural situations (Lücke, Kostova & Roth, 2014). This in turn makes them ideally equipped to act as agents of cross-cultural expertise in challenging workplace contexts, which require intercultural communication competencies (Moore & Barker, 2012).

To be more specific, their behaviour is guided by multiple cultural schemas (Bell & Harrison, 1996). This behavioural ambidexterity (Friedman & Liu, 2009) could increase multiculturals' ability to not only make "culturally appropriate interpretations" (Fitzsimmons, Miska & Stahl, 2011: 202), but also to change their behaviour according to the encountered cultural primes, a process also known as cultural frame switching (CFS) (Benet-Martinez et al., 2006). CFS is a mechanism by which culturally competent persons who have internalized two or more cultural value systems, change their "interpretive lenses in response to cultural cues" (Benet-Martinez & Haritatos, 2005: 1018). This switching mechanism, in which different behavioural repertoires are implemented according to certain cultural cues (Friedman & Liu, 2009), requires a solid knowledge and understanding in the ways of culture specific systems (Hong, 2010).

Multiculturals' abilities can also go beyond the cultural specific level and potentially develop into culture general skills, i.e. high levels of cultural metacognition (Hong, 2010). Cultural metacognition is the ability to consciously control one's mental and behavioural changes in a cross-cultural interaction (Brannen & Thomas, 2010). The development of these cultural general capabilities requires the ability to generalize from culture specific experiences and translate these into wider ranging behavioural systems (Lücke et al., 2014) as culture general skills "build on pre-existing knowledge, experience, and expertise" (Stadler, 2017: 451). Therefore, by developing a less contextual based behavioural repertoire, multiculturals might also possess the ability to cross-culturally code-switch even in culturally unfamiliar situations.

With MNCs being not only multicultural, but also multilingual entities (Luo & Shenkar, 2006), also language disparities can create operational challenges (Harzing, Köster & Magner, 2011; Marschan-Piekkari, Welch & Welch, 1999). As language carries social meanings (Kassis-Henderson, Cohen & McCulloch, 2018), language competency is usually a salient component of multicultural competence (LaFromboise, Coleman & Gerton, 1993). Furthermore, since multiculturals are often fluent in their respective languages (Furusawa & Brewster, 2015), they can perform not only the role of cultural translators or mediators, but also fulfil the role of language interpreters (Thomas, 2016). For example, the multiple language fluencies of multiculturals can be effectively used to prevent losses in translation within MNCs (Hong & Doz, 2013). Therefore, they are well suited to intervene in linguistically diverse settings.

Just as the culture specific skills can be used as a steppingstone in the development of culture general skills, language specific skills can equally carry with themselves the possibility of developing into language general skills. Language general skills refer to the capability to perceive and express nuances in a given communication style (Cohen et al., 2015). As such, they have been viewed as a set of dynamic interacting dimensions consisting of "knowledge, cross-cultural abilities, behavioural adaptability and cross-cultural communication skills, linked by CFS and cultural metacognition" (Mughan, 2015: 109).

While there is a certain preponderance in the multiculturalism literature to focus on multicultural identity development and multicultural characteristics, the outcomes of multiculturalism and multilingualism also deserve exploration (Dau, 2016), particularly their effects on multinational organizations (Fitzsimmons, 2013; Furusawa & Brewster, 2015). Our study is intended to investigate organizational outcomes of one particular group of multiculturals, i.e. highly skilled migrants. Furthermore, we decided to treat cultural and language skills as "conceptually distinct, but related and complementary" (Barner-Rasmussen, Ehrnrooth, Koveshnikov & Mäkelä, 2014: 890). As such, we look into both cultural and language (specific and general) skills that highly qualified migrants employ in a diverse working context.

3.2.2 Highly qualified migrants

As described above, multiculturals seem to enjoy a wide array of valuable skills, from cultural to linguistic, and from specific to general. One way to become multicultural is through migration (Vora, Martin, Fitzsimmons, Pekerti, Lakshman & Raheem, 2019) since a migration process brings with itself the adaptation to new cultural and linguistic contexts (Berry, 1997). As a result of this adaptation process, migrants can develop the ability to use differing behavioural repertoires, depending on the cultural context with which they come into contact (Bierbrauer & Klinger, 2005), or even become fluent in multiple languages (Nguyen & Benet-Martinez, 2007). If MNCs intend to take advantage of those cultural repertoires and language skills, they should employ migrants, for example, to fulfil boundary spanning roles (Hong & Doz, 2013). Nevertheless, in order for them to be recognized as boundary spanners and use their skills accordingly, migrants should also get into sufficiently influential positions for them to be able to employ their unique skills (Kane & Levina, 2017). Given that many of today's migrants are often highly skilled (Thomas, 2016), this should also increasingly be the case.

The focus of most migration studies has been on migrants who predominantly came from low social classes in their home countries (Crul & Doomernik, 2003; Thomson & Crul, 2007) and undertook in their host countries unskilled jobs such as low wage labor in manufacturing, construction and agriculture (Portes & Fernandes-Kelly, 2008), or domestic work (Berry & Bell, 2012). By contrast, more recent literature described also the influx of highly qualified migrants. This highly qualified mobile workforce usually holds a tertiary education degree (Iredale, 2001) and occupies jobs in engineering, programming, the medical field (Portes & Fernandez-Kelly, 2008), or managerial positions (Mattoo, Neagu & Özden, 2008).

The differences between high and low skilled migrants goes further than the educational background. Higher education has been found to be associated with lower integration stress (Beiser et al., 1988) and better adjustment to the host culture (Polek et al., 2008). Therefore, migrants with a high educational level also tend to identify themselves more with the receiving society (Recchi & Nebe, 2003). Furthermore, the level of education and mainstream language fluency are greatly interlinked as higher educated migrants tend to linguistically adapt better in their receiving society (Yagmur & van der Vijver, 2012). As most studies on migration have been conducted at a societal level, there appears to be a need to devote more attention to the individual level, particularly regarding highly qualified migrants (Hajro, Zilinskaite & Stahl, 2017).

3.2.3 Generational differences among highly skilled migrants

We argue that an investigation of highly skilled migrants' use of their multicultural and multilingual skills in MNCs should also consider their generational status as a relevant differentiator. Adjustment to another country is a complex process which encompasses elements such as language acquisition, behavioral integration, and possibly even identity change (Bakker, van der Zee & van Oudenhoven, 2006; Simon & Ruhs, 2008). Age of migration, i.e. age of arrival in the new country, significantly impacts the assimilation, acculturation, and economic success of migrants (Berg & Eckstein, 2009). If raised in both ethnic and mainstream cultures, children of migrants can also become multiculturals (Fitzsimmons, 2013; Levitt, 2009). As such, a distinction between first and second generation migrants is needed when discussing their role in MNCs.

The first generation of migrants is defined by migration research as those migrants being born in a country different from the receiving or so-called mainstream country (Gong, 2007). By contrast, the second-generation of migrants is understood as the offspring of first generation migrants who are born and grown up in the mainstream society (Heath, Rothon & Kilpi, 2008; Worbs, 2003). The first generation tends to keep the ethnic language, i.e. home country language, as dominant (Yagmur & van de Vijver, 2012), whereas the second generation usually grows up bilingually (Fitzsimmons, 2013). In addition, the differing migrant generations also experience contrasting identity formation processes. The first generation tends to identify more with the ethnic country, and the second generation with both ethnic and mainstream culture (Fitzsimmons, 2013). Pertaining to their multicultural skills, Martin & Shao (2016) make the distinction between achieved and innate multiculturalism. Achieved multiculturals have experienced the cultural immersion process at a later stage in their life. As such, an example for achieved multiculturals would be the first generation migrants. This view concurs with Lücke & Roth (2008) who state that multiculturalism can be developed through social experiences at a later point in life. Innate multiculturals on the other hand are individuals who experience the cultural immersion at an early stage in their development, such as second generation migrants (Martin & Shao, 2016). The skills of highly qualified migrants and the use of these multicultural and multilingual skills in a multinational working environment have seldom been the focus of empirical studies (Benson-Rea & Rawlinson, 2003). Furthermore, since first and second generation of highly qualified migrants can also be categorized into achieved and innate multiculturals, we intend to address this gap that appears to us of both conceptual and practical relevance. Hence, we intend to exploratively investigate the following research question: *how do first and second generation highly skilled migrants differ in their multicultural and multilingual skills which they apply in an international work context?*

3.3 Methodology

3.3.1 Research design

To our knowledge, a systematic investigation of the cultural skills and language skills of highly qualified migrants in a multicultural-multilingual working environment has not yet been undertaken. As such, we employed an inductive, explorative approach to address our research question and generate new theory (Siggelkow, 2007). As our topic has not been conceptualized in depth in previous studies, we employed a theory generating approach (Suddaby, 2006). This approach allowed us to explore *"how"* and *"why"* questions more in depth (Pratt, 2009) and collect rich content data based on our interviewees' close experiences (Gioia, Corley & Hamilton, 2013). In concurrence with Siggelkow (2007), and Eisenhardt & Graebner (2007), we grounded our investigation in prior research, mainly stemming from the areas of cross-cultural management and migration studies. Although our initial research guided us towards constructs such as cultural and language skills, and generational differences of migrants, we remained open towards our interviewees' disclosure on *how* they used their skills and *why* the generations differ from each other in their skill usage (Eisenhardt, 1989). After various rounds of iterations between data collection, data analysis and literature review we noticed the interplay between culture specific and culture general, resp. language specific and language general skills on one side, and generational status on the other. This observation prompted us to extend our research into lines of investigation we had previously not considered (Edmondson & McManus, 2007). Based on the analysis of our explorative data, we aimed at developing a mid-range theory. While only applicable to a limited conceptual range (Merton, 1968) but small enough to be studied in depth, mid-range theories allow researchers to address issues large enough to make a significant contribution (Daft & Lewin, 1993; Eisenhardt, 1989).

3.3.2 Research setting

In order to keep the working country context constant and better be able to compare results, we conducted our investigation in a single country: Germany. Germany is of particular interest since it has known a continuous influx of migrants since the first waves of "guest workers" in the 1950s. This has led to a migrant population of 21.2 million (Statistisches Bundesamt, 2020), out of which 10.1 million are first generation migrants, and 11.1 million second generation migrants. This substantial migration influx allows for the study of generational differences. Furthermore, being one of the most advanced economies of the European Union, Germany presents extensive educational and professional opportunities, including for highly skilled migrants. Due to Germany's international economic relevance and to the highly export-oriented nature of Germany's industries, German companies feature a considerable amount of international operations all across the value chain. Therefore, we expect the interplay between international business activities taking place in German MNCs and the employment of highly qualified migrants of first and second generation to yield interesting results.

For our specific research purposes, we had several sampling criteria. Firstly, we looked for highly qualified migrants working for multinational companies. We searched for both, first and second generation migrants in order to establish potential differences and/or commonalities between these two groups (see Table 1). Secondly, since underemployment is a challenging reality even for highly qualified migrants (Al Ariss & Crowley-Henry, 2013), we specifically selected only those candidates who had positions according to their level of education and professional qualifications. Thirdly, to increase the robustness of our findings (Miles & Huberman, 1994), we ensured that our respondents were of a large variety of ethnical backgrounds and worked in a broad variety of industries and functional areas. The diversity of our respondents' ethnical backgrounds is depicted in Table 1, the wide range of industries they work for in Table 2 and the spread of their workplaces in Table 3. This multidimensional diversity enabled us to identify results replicated across different industries or functional areas (Eisenhardt & Graebner, 2007), thus strengthening the robustness of our mid-range theory building. All interviews were face-to-face, except for a few interviews held via telephone or Skype.

Table 1. Interviewees according to ethnic background across both generations

Generational status	Ethnic background (countries)	Number of interviews
First generation	Argentina, Australia, Bolivia, Brazil, China, Colombia, Croatia, France, Hungary, India, Iran, Italy, Lithuania, Mexico, Netherlands, Mexico, Pakistan, Palestine, Peru, Poland, Romania, Russia, Senegal, South Africa, Spain, Taiwan, Thailand, Turkey, United Kingdom, United States of America, Venezuela	58
Second generation	Algeria, Argentina, Bosnia, Brazil, Bulgaria, Canada, China, Croatia, France, Greece, Italy, India, Kazakhstan, Lebanon, Mexico, Palestine, Peru, Philippines, Poland, Romania, Russia, Serbia, Slovakia, South Africa, South Korea, Sri Lanka, Sweden, Turkey, United Kingdom, United States of America, Vietnam	72
Total		130

Table 2. Interviewees according to the industries in which they work

Industry	Number of interviews
Aerospace	1
Automotive producer	14
Automotive supplier	26
Bank	7
Car sharing	2
Construction	1
Consulting	5
Energy	1
Exhibition planning	1
Fashion	8
Floriculture	1
Food processing	1
Healthcare	4
Hotel	1
Household entertainment technology	1
Household products	2
Industrial and mechanical engineering	7
Insurance	2
Medical services	8
Music apparel	1

Table 3. Interviewees according to the functional areas in which they work

Functional area	Number of interviews
Accounting	2
Business Analysis	13
Architecture	1
Assistance	15
CEO	1
Consulting	1
Controlling	2
Customer care/service	8
Data management	1
Design	1
Distribution	1
Division management	2
Human resources	7
IT	4
Logistics	1
Executive management	1
Marketing	3
Product and business development	1
Product engineering	36
Product management	1
Purchasing	8
Quality management and sales	1
Regulatory	1
Research	4

No industry mention	3
Pharmacology	4
Professional training	2
Real estate	2
Research centre	4
Software development	11
Technology services	2
Temporary employment	1
Textile	3
Transportation	2
Wholesale	2

Research and customer care	1
Research and division management	1
Sales	10
Sales and production	1
Software consulting	1
Textile engineering	1

3.3.3 Data collection

Our data set consists of 130 semi-structured interviews conducted between 2015 and 2018. The semi-structured interview is a highly efficient method to collect rich data, as it allows participants to predominantly reflect on critical incidents from their working environments (Hajro & Pudelko, 2010). On one side, the semi-structured interview facilitates in-depth learning about the perceptions and reactions of the individual interviewees by means of specific follow-up questions (Weiss, 1994), and on the other side it allows for the comparability between the interviews, through asking similar key questions. Moreover, by keeping the order of our questions flexible, our respondents were able to keep the train of their thoughts. As such, we managed to receive detailed insights into our interviewees' individual experiences and perspectives, and to contrast and evaluate them against one another. Furthermore, by doing semi-structured interviews, we could investigate previously unanticipated issues (Myers, 2008). For example, we initially did not consider making the distinction between culture specific and culture general, or language specific and language general skills. However, by employing semi-structured interviews, we soon became aware of the use of skills transcending the own ethnic background. As a result, we incorporated questions about this skill variation into our interview guideline. Subsequently, we discovered differences along this general skill dimension between the first and second generation of highly qualified migrants.

The interviews consisted of open-ended questions, allowing for an in-depth investigation of our respondents' perceptions and the clarification of unclear accounts (Witzel, 2000). Our interview guideline was organized according to standard procedures for semi-structured interviews (Brinkmann & Kvale, 2015) and consisted of four sections. We started the interviews with general background information about the respondents' age, nationality, generational status in relation to the migration to Germany, years of stay and work in Germany (1st generation migrants only), reasons for migration (1st generation migrants only). The second part focused on aspects such as cultural identity or language preferences. The following section pertained to more job-related aspects, as we solicited information regarding their educational background, position and tasks at work. The fourth and most extensive part of the interview was designed to explore the use of cultural and language skills at work. In this section we firstly focused on the use of their culture and language specific skills and subsequently we enquired about the use of culture and language general skills at work. We particularly asked for extensive and rich descriptions in support of our in-depth information gathering. Here, we particularly focused on questions such as "In what context do you use other languages at work?", "How often do you use (e.g.) Turkish at work?", "How much contact do you have with third cultures at work?", or "What steps do you make in order to improve the communication with the (e.g.) Russian subsidiary?"

To achieve investigator triangulation, 69 out of the 130 interviews were conducted by 13 master's students within the context of an applied qualitative research seminar. The migratory background of the first author, who did 61 out of 130 interviews and trained the master's students who did the remaining 69, was of advantage for conducting and analysing the interviews. Being a highly qualified migrant in Germany herself who has grown up with two cultures and languages, she could easily establish a closer initial rapport with the migrant respondents and show empathy with them during the interviews. As a result, interviewees felt free to provide rich accounts of their experiences and to openly discuss culturally and linguistically challenging situations at the workplace. In order to ensure consistency across all interviews and construct validity, the first author designed the interview guideline, applied it in her first interviews and subsequently discussed it in detail with her master's students (Sinkovics, Penz & Ghauri, 2008). This made the comparison and contrasting of findings possible, thus decreasing potential bias in the interpretation of the results (Denzin, 2017; Yeung, 1995).

The interviews were conducted in the language choice of the participants, allowing them to speak at most ease (Harzing & Maznevski, 2002), if the language skills of the interviewers permitted. These included English, Spanish, and Romanian, but most interviews were held in German as Germany was also the country all interviewees lived and worked in. Interviews lasted 1 hour on average with the shortest interview taking 31 minutes and the longest interview 1 hour and 33 minutes. All interviews were tape recorded and transcribed verbatim which resulted in 1650 pages of double-spaced data. The transcriptions were done in the original language of the interview to maintain the contextual sense of the interviewees' statements (Bell & Bryman, 2007; Squires, 2009). As both authors speak German as their mother tongue and the first author has a working proficiency in the other three interview languages, resp. English, Spanish, and Romanian, the authenticity of the respondents' perspective could be maintained (Langley, 1999; Squires, 2009). By contrast, subsequent coding was done in English, and the quotations we used for illustration purposes in this paper were translated in English if necessary.

3.3.4 Data analysis

Coding was done mainly by the first author. For reliability purposes, the 13 master's students independently coded their transcripts. Their coding was subsequently compared with the first author's coding. In case of differing coding, the emerging codes and categories were extensively discussed until reliability was satisfactory. We followed Gioia et al. (2013) and Locke (2001) in already analysing the first interviews, while still collecting data. Data analysis was done with help of the coding software Atlas.ti. Some codes were taken directly from the data. For example, the quote "I would actually identify myself as European" was coded as "identifies as European". Other codes, which marked already existing theoretical concepts, were taken from the literature. For example, the quote "Indian subsidiary gave more information" resulted in the code "more intensive knowledge exchange with ethnic subsidiary". Throughout the interviews and the coding processes, we continuously iterated between data collection, data analysis and literature study (Glaser & Strauss, 1967; Locke, 2001). Table 4 provides an illustration of additional quotes and ensuing first order codes.

Table 4. Quotes from the interviews and first order codes

Examples of interview quotations	First order concepts
Because my current company has a lot of Indians in it, when I am speaking to those colleagues, it is mostly Hindi. It is more comfortable. (first generation, India, 16072018)	Speaks ethnic language with ethnic subsidiary
I think the markets feel that they can communicate better with me. Some of them speak Chinese with me every day or try to write me in Chinese every day. (first generation, Taiwan, 02102018)	Speaks ethnic language with ethnic markets
Only with Korean subsidiary colleagues…I think that my relationship with them is rather good. If I need something or when something is needed, they rapidly send it. And when my colleagues here needed something from the Koreans, they would ask me to tell them. (first generation, Iran, 06062016)	Culture general information exchange with foreign subsidiaries

Although I was only the intern there, due to my communication changes, foreign subsidiary colleagues began adressing me by my first name. They knew who I was and I made a good impression. (second generation, Russia, 29032916, TR)	Culture general communication with foreign subsidiaries
If the clients knew little German, they would nod more than talk. And when I intervened and talked to them in Turkish, they would often say 'oh, so this is what they meant to say'. (second generation, Turkey, 26092015, TR)	Improvement of communication when language specific proficiency is low
And then, if I speak with people who don't speak English that well, I use simpler words. (second generation, Malaysia, 15082015, TR)	Language general communication improvement

Our analysis comprised three consecutive levels of data aggregation. First, we carefully went through each passage of our interviews and tagged each relevant statement with an appropriate first order code. At this stage, we applied Strauss & Corbin's (1998) method of open coding, as we remained close to our respondents' perceptions (Gioia et al., 2013). In order to reduce the amount of first order codes to a feasible number (Gioia et al., 2013) and make more conceptual sense out of them, we then proceeded by employing the constant comparative method (Glaser & Strauss, 1967) to aggregate codes into more conceptual categories and ultimately into theoretical constructs (Lee, 1999). First, we compared different parts of each interview to ensure consistency. Subsequently, we contrasted interviews with first generation migrants with those conducted with second generation migrants, paying particular attention to similarities and dissimilarities. At this stage, we also noticed different patterns when it came to culture general and language general skills. This appeared to us as a phenomenon that was explained as such in the literature but derived from our coding efforts of the 1650 pages of transcripts. We also searched for patterns when comparing interviews across industries and functional areas but could not arrive at any meaningful differentiations from which we concluded that these two dimensions were of less relevance when describing the application of particular skills of first and second generation migrants. Through this constant comparative method, we moved from a primarily descriptive to a more conceptual level of codes (Van Laer & Janssens, 2011). For example, the codes "using ethnic language with ethnic markets" and "intensive contact with ethnic market due to language" were consolidated into the second-order code "ethnic language communication node". Finally, we aggregated the second-order codes into conceptual building blocks (Myers, 2008). Following Gioia et al. (2013), we visualized our data structure (see Figure 1). During this entire process of analysis, we continuously refined the emerging theory from our data until a saturation point was reached and no new information could be derived from the interpretation of our data (Locke, 2001).

Figure 1. Examples of codes, second order concepts and theoretical building blocks

Examples of first order codes   Second order codes   Conceptual building blocks

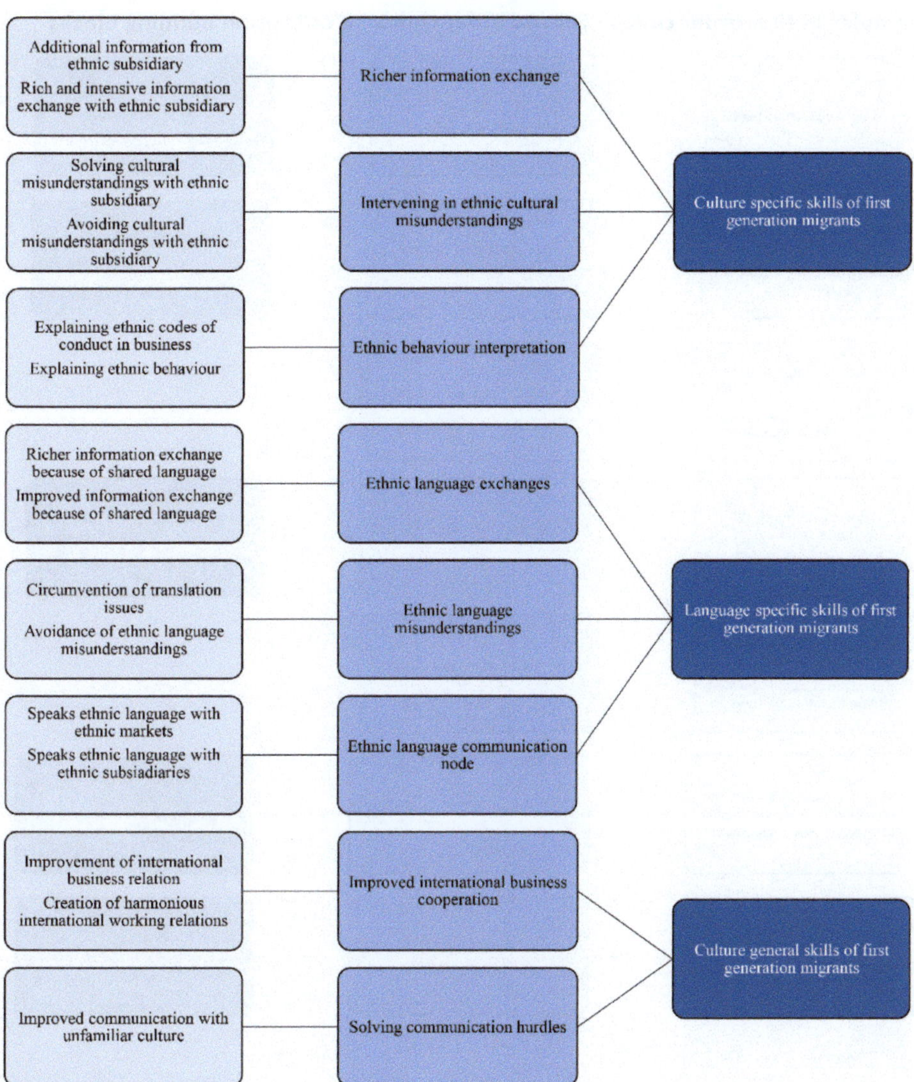

Figure 1. Examples of codes, second order concepts and theoretical building blocks (continued)

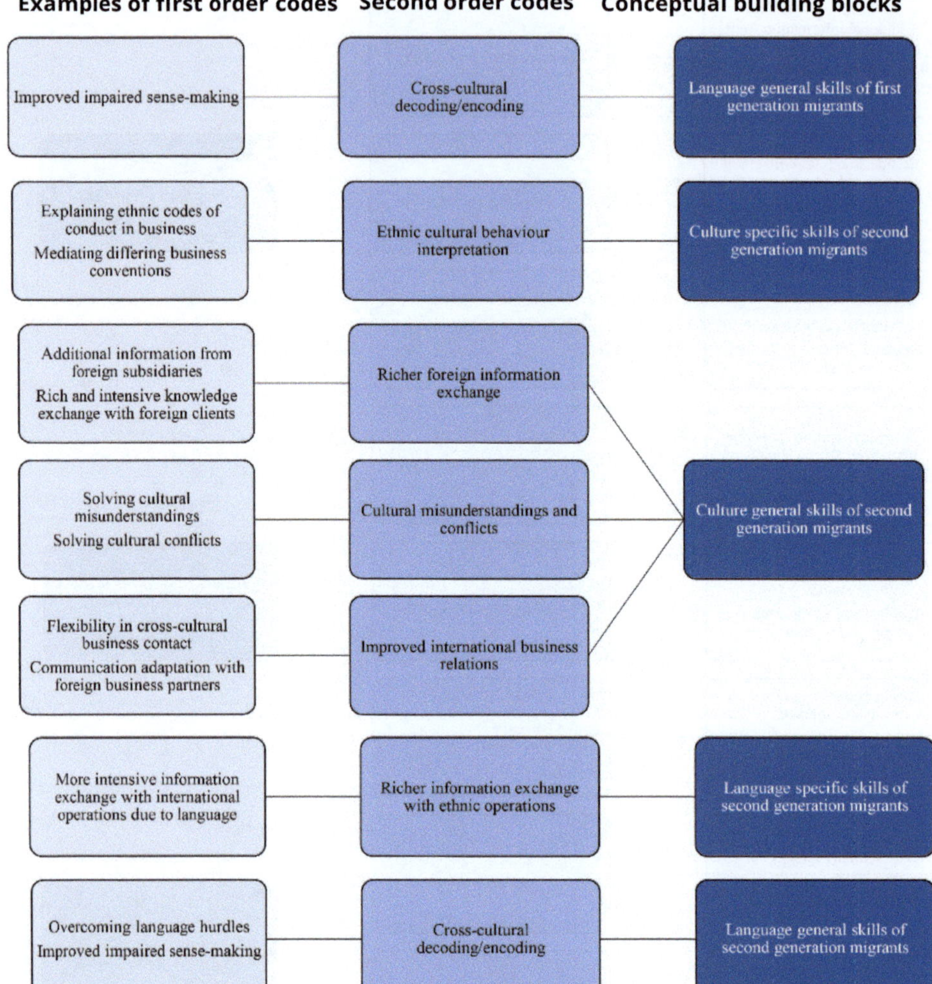

3.4 Findings

In the following, we outline our findings on the abilities of first and second generation highly qualified migrants to implement their cultural and language skills and thus create more positive outcomes in their multinational working environment by counteracting the adverse effects of cultural and linguistic diversity. In order to better illustrate the similarities and contrasts between first generation and second generation highly qualified migrants, we have structured our findings according to their cultural and language skills, focusing within each skill section on the generational particularities.

3.4.1 Culture-specific skills of highly qualified migrants

First generation migrants. Because first generation migrants change their national context at a later stage in their life, they continue to be highly influenced by their ethnic culture, even after migrating. Therefore, our interviewees related, for example, that when working at the headquarters of an MNC in their host country, it was relatively easy for them to access relevant information from subsidiaries of their ethnic country. This indispensable information would not have been so easily shared by subsidiary locals with HQ nationals.

> I would also get information [from the Indian subsidiary] about which one does not talk in the big meetings. Those things from behind the curtains … I get those very easily because I have a connection with the people. If some German would be doing the same job, he would never get that information. (first generation, India, 25022016)

Our finding concurrs with Hong's (2010) suggestion that a shared meaning system can effectively lead to an improved knowledge or information transfer.

Furthermore, because of their ethnic cultural proficiency, first generation migrants were also able to correctly interpret business actions or working processes of locals from ethnic country subsidiaries.

> And what I could add would be that I better understand the working culture of Hungarians. This helps me in assessing why some things

take more or less time or why some things are done a certain way; I can understand the background better. (first generation, Hungary, 25012018, TR)

Thus, by properly explaining certain behaviours or working cultures, first generation migrants were able to act as efficient behavioural intrepreters and improve the collaboration between mainstream and ethnic business operations, supporting similar findings by Nahapiet & Ghoshal (1998). Furthermore, our first generation interviewees were also able to resolve certain cross-cultural disputes.

There were some times when I felt like the situation was escalating, because of the misinformation or the misunderstandings [with the Romanian subsidiary]. There were at least two or three situations in which I felt I can help to resolve an issue that was about to get out of control, to escalate. (first generation, Romania, 19022016)

First generation migrants, being fully proficient in their ethnic culture, naturally possess culture-specific competencies and knowledge, and are therefore ideal cross-cultural mediators. Our findings thus support those of Nguyen & Benet-Martinez (2007) and Fitzsimmons et al. (2011), who reported that multicultural individuals are able to sense conflictuous situations and intervene by acting as cross-cultural mediators.

Taking into consideration our findings pertaining to the culture specific skills of our first generation highly qualified migrant respondents and their application in a multinational work context, we propose the following:

Proposition 1a:
First generation highly qualified migrants possess culture specific skills which they employ to improve work outcomes with ethnic business operations.

However, it seems that first generation migrants still have some difficulties or a certain uneasiness with mainstream work process and/or behaviour.

For example, when we have a project and we are trying to find to a solution and we are not quite sure about how it would work. I would say take a risk and choose option A. B could also be good but nobody wants to make this decision. Through my Indian culture I am used to trying out a lot of stuff. If I try out 10 new ideas and 6 work out, then this a good average for me. I think that the German culture is different. One does only three things but perfectly…I have noticed that mistakes are hardly accepted here. And this leads to less courage to try out new ideas. (first generation, India, 17052016, TR)

I regularly have to remember to draw a line between the private and the professional sphere. It is sometimes difficult because emotions do surface and there is the tendency to mix them up…or when I write about processes and I automatically do some steps in my mind. And then a colleague says that steps are missing. So they need everything detailed and written precisely. These are situations where I realize that I have to think German – this means define more and write everything. (first generation, Iran, 060602016, TR)

Considering first generation migrants' upbringing in their ethnic countries and their late relocation (Fitzsimmons, 2013), this persistent ethnic domination in their behaviour or mindset comes at no surprise. Nevertheless, it seems that this deep ethnic influence could potentially be a detriment for their own work outcomes. In light of these findings, we propose the following:

Proposition 1b:
First generation highly qualified migrants' ingrained ethnic mindset can negatively impact own work outcomes within mainstream work processes.

Pertaining to the first generation, we thus find that due to their proficient culture specific skills, they are well suited to improve the information transfer between the mainstream and ethnic operations, correctly interpret ethnic behaviour, and also solve or avoid cross-cultural disputes. However, their deeply rooted ethnic mindset could potentially undermine their own work outcomes in the mainstream company context.

*Second generation migrant.*We went on investigating the particularities of the second generation of highly qualified migrants as we wanted to explore their culture specific skills and how they apply them. Similar to the first generation highly qualified migrants, we found that the second generation was very active in interpreting for their mainstream country colleagues culture-specific actions or behaviours from ethnic country business operations, thereby facilitating cross-cultural business encounters. This sort of assistance was also very much demanded by their mainstream country colleagues. As a result of these interventions, second generation migrants were able to improve a mutual understanding in a fundamental way.

> If you send an email to a Brazilian colleague, he will only reply when he has the full solution instead of saying "I'm working on it". And even if they are delayed, they will not tell you. They just think they have to come back to you with the full solution and they don't even give you a sign that they read your email. And then the perception of the Germans is that the Brazilians don't care. I would tell the Brazilian colleagues to at least tell that they are working on it or to let us know if they are late. That might seem obvious for someone working here. In this case it was an advantage to be able to give some hints about how to reply to emails because the Germans think you are not working on it at all. (second generation, Brazil, 16122016)

> I would relate this to my cultural background. I can better understand situations in which Russian colleagues don't show initiative or don't respond. This does not mean that they are not motivated, but maybe they lack the courage, due to the respect they have towards the German colleagues, or to say that it is too complicated for them. In this case they wait until the German side contacts them. (second generation, Russia, 22062016, TR)

It became evident that second generation migrants, who had usually been raised in a multicultural environment, are highly competent decoders of culturally differing behavioral cues such as, for example, punctuality, work processes or hierarchical expectations. Our findings resonate with existing research (Backmann, Kanitz, Tian, Hoffmann & Hoegl, 2020; Kane & Levina, 2017) that migrants can effectively use their proficient ethnic culture knowledge to build bridges between mainstream and ethnic operations.

Furthermore, comparing responses from first and second generation migrants, we understood that second generation migrants used their culture specific skills in a much broader array of situations, many of them taking place in rather informal or sporadical situations.

> I communicate with the Italian colleagues maybe one or two times per month. It depends on how many problems they have and who is actually the contact person, so from which department. (second generation, Italy,15072016, TR)

Our findings support studies by Barner-Rasmussen, Ehrnrooth, Koveshnikov & Mäkelä (2014) and Blazejewski (2012) who argued that effective cross-cultural assistance can also be provided by organizational members in non-leadership positions and that the use of their abilities might have more of an intrinsic motivation rather than a motivation related to their organizational position and tasks. Based on these findings, we propose the following:

Proposition 1c:
Second generation highly qualified migrants possess culture specific skills which they employ to improve work outcomes with ethnic business operations.

We further found that second generation migrants' early immersion in two (or more) cultures provided them with a high degree of cultural sensitivity which Martin & Shao (2016: 15) labeled as "a balance in cultural knowledge", something that first generation migrants, with their much belated exposure to the mainstream culture, did not have to this extent.

> The Arabic culture does not play any role in the professional sphere. The Arabic culture which I enjoy in private, with its lack of punctuality and chaotic style, would not be suitable for work here. (second generation, Lebanon, 18122015, TR)

> At work I have to slow down the Turkish quick temper. (second generation, Turkey, 26092015, TR)

> It depends on whether one looks at the private or professional sphere. At my workplace, I have to be German, [company name]is a German company, the majority is German. In private, the situation is more colourful, all three cultures are represented. (second generation, Austria-France, 25012018, TR)

It seems that the second generation, compared with the first generation, are better able at compartmentalizing their cultures if needed. This would concur with the notion of CFS (Benet-Martinez & Haritatos, 2005) that skilled multiculturals are able to adapt their behaviour in response to the cultural cues which they encounter. We thus propose the following:

Proposition 1d:
Second generation highly qualified migrants have a higher ability compared to first generation migrants to compartmentalize their ethnic and mainstream culture skill sets and to draw on the one or the other when needed.

Overall, we found it interesting to observe that second-generation migrants were even better able to assist in encounters with members of their ethnic culture, and this even though first generation migrants have an even more intimate knowledge of the culture in which they grew up. Apparently, being a second-generation migrant provides organizational members with an equi-distance in relation to their cultures that puts them in the unique position to facilitate relations between business representatives of their cultures.

3.4.2   Language-specific skills of highly qualified migrants

First generation migrants. Since multinational companies are confronted not only with challenges related to cultural diversity, but also with issues stemming from their inherent language diversity, we further looked into the language-specific skills that our first generation respondents employed. We found that their language specific skills enabled them to substantially improve the flow of information between various mainstream and ethnic stakeholders.

> Yes, especially when the language level of the others is not that good or when it comes to technical and complex subject matters, such as IT

projects, I can be of assistance. They [Polish employees, responsible for IT support] feel uncomfortable to do it in English because they are unsure how it would be understood, or that it comes to a misunderstanding. In this case, it is easier for them to say it first to me in Polish; this way, they are sure that they are understood properly. (first generation, Poland, 17062017, TR)

As our first generation interviewees strongly emphasized, being fluent ethnic language speakers (Yagmur & van de Vijver, 2012), they can employ their specific language skills to reduce linguistic barriers between various stakeholders. In addition, our data also clearly show that the use of a corporate language is not necessarily the panacea for language problems in MNCs. Hence, our findings support other studies on how a corporate language, in most cases English (Harzing & Pudelko, 2013), can lead to new sets of problems, such as power distortions (Tenzer & Pudelko, 2017; Yanaprasart, 2015) or fluency assymetries (Fiedler, 2010). Consequently, we found that by placing first generation migrants as connecting and communication nodes, linguistic hurdles in the communication flow processes can be significantly reduced.

When working at X [company name] we were doing customer support at an international level. We also had customers from Russia, from Sibiria. There were some communication issues with them and I was asked to intervene and help. By talking Russian, we could talk in detail about solutions. (first generation, Russia, 21092018, TR)

According to our data, the most often occuring negative outcome stemming from language differences in working contexts were misunderstandings. If not solved on time or properly, misunderstandings could easily escalate into major disputes. First generation migrants were able to interve in these situations and help avoid conflicts.

We have a subsidiary in Poland and during a conversation with them there was a situation which could have led to misunderstandings but I managed to catch it on time. (first generation, Poland, 25012018, TR)

Based on our interviews, we conclude that first generation migrants certainly possess the appropriate ethnic language repertoire which helps them "reduce the number of misunderstandings, thus minimizing conflicts and tension" (Barner-Rasmussen et al., 2014: 891). Based on these findings, we propose the following:

Proposition 2a:
First generation highly qualified migrants possess language specific skills which they employ to improve work outcomes with ethnic business operations.

In spite of the work benefits related to their ethnic language proficiency, first generation migrants still seem to struggle with the mainstream language.

But still, sometimes I'm missing some words, technical words. (first generation, India, 25022016)

Because I work in German, it sometimes takes me longer to expresss myself than my colleagues who are native speakers. (first generation, Spain, 22042018 , TR)

I sometimes find it difficult to explain the situation in a professional manner. It can then happen that colleagues ask me what I am trying to say...so I believe that my language level [German] was not sufficient in some situations. (first generation, Russia, 15042017, TR)

Although studies have shown that a higher educational level is usually associated with a better language adjustment in the receiving country (Yagmur & van der Vijver, 2012), this linguistic integration takes time. Hence, first generation migrants sometimes perceive their level of the mainstream language as insufficient by contrast to native speakers. This flawed proficiency of the mainstream language could in turn counterbalance the positive effects of their specific skills, respectively own work outcomes. We thus propose the following:

Proposition 2b:
First generation highly qualified migrants' insufficient mainstream language skills can negatively impact own work outcomes within mainstream work processes.

In spite of their mainstream language deficiencies, we found language-specific skills of first generation migrants to be of relevance in improving the flow of information exchange between international business operations, in overcoming linguistic hurdles, and in diffusing misunderstandings which could have seriously undermined cross-national business interactions.

As we wanted to juxtapose generations of highly qualified migrants and their skills, we also investigated the language specific skils of the *second generation*. Since second generation migrants are usually immersed in two (or more) cultures from beginning on, they also enjoy a multilingual upbringing (Fitzsimmons, 2013).

> At school we talked German, with my friends I talked more German than Turkish, and at home we talked only Turkish. (second generation, Turkey, 01102015, TR)

> At home we speak a mixture of German and Russian because it is simpler this way. (second generation, Russia, 10022016, TR)

As these sample quotes exemplify, second generation migrants integrated both languages very naturally in their every day lives (Fitzsimmons, 2013; Martin & Shao, 2016) and this to an extent that clearly exeeds the one of first generation migrants. This often almost perfect linguistic ambidexterity provides them with the ability to linguistically assist in situations in which the corporate language skills of various stakeholders prove to be insufficient. To be more specific, by using their ethnic language skills, they often enable a proper and efficient information exchange.

> At the beginning, my supervisor was holding the conferences with Russia in English and I was just making some remarks in the process. However, due to multiple problems, such as misunderstandings, I ended up doing all by myself in Russian and later on let my German

> colleagues know what we talked about. (second generation, Russia, 22062016, TR)

Similar to our findings pertaining to the first generation, we noticed also in this case that the use of a corporate language, in most cases English, did not guarantee communication across linguistic boundaries to be free of misunderstandings. In this context, second generation migrants, with their dual fluency, appear to be particularly well suited to overcome communication hurdles due to insufficient proficiency in the corporate language (Fiedler, 2010). We thus propopse the following:

Proposition 2c:
Second generation highly qualified migrants possess language specific skills which they employ to improve work outcomes with ethnic business operations.

We could additionally establish that particularly the second generation migrants' fluency in two languages did not only pertain to lexical or phonetic aspects.

> I think it's a huge advantage to really speak the language properly. I hear a lot of confusing instructions given by Germans because they're not comfortable enough with the language to know how to phrase something. Because my German colleagues' way of speaking is geared towards efficiency, clarity and communicating effectiveley. But you need the tools to do a fitting translation. (second generation, United Kingdom, 13102017)

We thus noticed in our interviews the relevance of pragmatic and prosodic cues to create meaning. Pragmatic cues are speech acts like apologizing, requesting or refusing, which follow culture-specific patterns, while prosodic cues refer to acoustic speech acts like loudness of the voice, intonation or speaking rhythm and speed (Wierzbicka, 2003). Second generation migrants were able not only to properly express themselves in writing and when speaking, but also to transfer and correctly interpret speech conventions, an ability that requires bilingual skills. Given their high proficiency in two languages, second generation migrants had evident advantages over first generation migrants. Due to these intergenerational differences, we propose the following:

Proposition 2d:
Second generation highly qualified migrants are better able than first generation migrants to alternate between their ethnic and mainstream languagees due to their comprehensive bilingual skills.

Consequently, we found first generation migrants to have ideal culture- and language-specific skills for creating a richer information exchange, intervening in impaired sensemaking situations, forming a shared narrative system, and overcoming possible conflict situations. By employing these skills, they are able to create positive outcomes in differing cross-cultural and -lingual business constellations. Our findings clearly demonstrate that second generation migrants enable information exchange by overcoming communication barriers stemming from insufficient skills in the corporate language. This makes them well suited to act as communication nodes between the mainstream and ethnic business operations.

Overall, we find that second generation migrants' ingrained cultural and linguistic ambidexterity allowed them to establish a perfect balance between two cultures and languages. On the flipside, first generation migrants, with their late exposure to the host country, are not able to develop such a cultural and linguistic balance.

3.4.3 Culture-general skills of highly qualified migrants

First generation migrants. The existence and relevance of culture- and language-*specific* skills of first generation migrants is not overly surprising: first generation migrants possess (and are generally assumed by colleagues, supervisors, and business partners to possess) a deep understanding of their ethnic culture and a perfect knowledge of their ethnic language, which they can put into practical use in the context of mainstream-ethnic international business operations. In comparison, more interesting have been our findings pertaining to culture-*general* skills (and subsequently language-*general* skills), i.e. skills used in culturally unfamiliar situations. According to Molinsky (2007), culture-general skills pertain to the ability to deviate from the embedded cultural patterns and engage in a behaviour which is accepted in a culturally unfamilar context. On the basis of our interviews, we not only found evidence for *first generation* migrants' helpful use of their intimate knowledge of their own specific culture, but also for the ability to employ a more general cultural understanding in dealing with people from culturally unknown countries.

> After eight years working in Germany, I noticed how my multiculturalism can be a general advantage. It was when my supervisor sent me to the Czech Republic because that team needed some urgent help. They were actually really in a bad state and they were not motivated. They were in a kind of a non-cooperative situation ... I was trying to emotionally connect with them and they were able to talk to me openly about what was going on. And when I came back, my supervisor was like: "Wow! What you did was something we have been trying to do for months, but we couldn't get through to them." They were really amazed, they did not really know what had happened... My supervisor and his supervisor were always keeping a distance to the Czechs, they were always trying to be more careful in how they talked with them, and they were not trying to really connect with them or trying to understand their problem. And I think I broke the ice, because the Czech colleagues' kind of assumed that anybody who comes from Germany is going to be like that. And that is something they actually told me. I think I automatically switched and opened up to a different mentality and I wanted to actually understand what was going on. (first generation, India, 02102018)

This culture-general capability to relate to members of an unfamiliar culture could be compared with a higher order metacognition (Barner-Rasmussen, 2015) or with cultural intelligence (CQ) (Thomas et al., 2015), and is based on prior experiences with another culture. These skills are difficult to pinpoint (Stadler, 2017) because they entail aspects such as open-mindedness, a feature which is generally believed to characterize multicultural individuals (Moore & Barker, 2012; Van der Zee & Van Oudenhoven, 2000). Besides their difficulty in defining and proving them, culture general skills are also highly complex and difficult to acquire (Stadler, 2017).

In the instances in which our first generation interviewees reported that they had the occasion to improve working outcomes in culturally unfamiliar contexts, they most often engaged in improving (cultural) communication.

> When we were in video conferences with South Korea, and in the room we had a lot of Germans, I had to basically moderate the discussion between the German colleagues on one side and the Koreans on the other, so that they understood each other. I soon realized that they were basically judging each other from their own perspective, so I had to step in and say, "No, no, you are not listening to each other. Can you explain it again?" And I was kind of doing a translation. Not a language translation but a cultural translation. (first generation, France, 17032017)

As the above quote suggests, first generation migrants are particularly able to detect where certain communication asymmetries arise and step in to mediate. Such cultural-general skills enable migrants to take on the role of an "universal encoder/decoder": one needs to have a basic understanding of a cultural background in order to "encode/decode" a message appropriately, otherweise one runs the risk of using a common corporate language but with different meaning systems (see also Fujio, 2004; Steyaert, Ostendorp & Gaibrois, 2011). First generation migrants seem to have the cognitive ability of learning from their international experience and become skilled at intrepreting messages from a culturally unfamiliar context.

Building on our respondents' assertions, we furthermore found that first generation migrants were able to avoid dissensions within their organizations, by supporting a more harmonious working atmosphere.

> I began by emphasizing that we are a team and that we have a common goal. And then I said that we will manage this together and only as a team. Germans would not have done something like this. I showed empathy by listening to them [Japanese] because for them, the team is the be-all and end-all. This way they felt taken seriously and their values respected. (first generation, France, 22022016, TR)

Our interviews clearly suggest that even if first generation migrants are primed with culturally unfamiliar cues, they are able to develop abilities which would bring their cultural dexterity to an universally valid level. This supports the more general argument by Beechler, Søndergaard, Miller & Bird (2004: 125) who argue that an effective cross-cultural negotiator possesses the "explicit and tacit knowledge of how to do things, what to do … and why something is important". Taking these findings into account, we propose the following:

Proposition 3a:
First generation migrants possess cultural general skills which they employ to improve work outcomes in culturally unknown work situations.

Our findings thus provide evidence for a potentially universal form of code-switching, in which first generation migrants modify their behaviour in order to accommodate to a foreign setting (see also Molinsky, 2007). First generation migrants seem to be able to connect with culturally unknown stakeholders and thus improve the information exchange, communication and general work atmosphere. However, since we noticed that only certain interviewees mentioned being able to adapt to culturally unknown situations, we made use of the advantages of our qualitative research path to look more closely at the specific characteristics of our first generation respondents who ascertained that they were effective cultural mediators in culturally unknown situations. We thus found that those interviewees who spent a considerable amount of time in the mainstream country (i.e. more than 5 years) were able to develop certain culture-general abilities. It is believed that five years is the minimum time one has to spend in the mainstream country in order to assimilate (Benet-Martinez & Haritatos, 2005; Kane & Levina, 2017). According to our findings, this is also the minimum time one needs to experience a different cultural environment in order to develop culture-general skills. In light of these outcomes, we propose the following:

Proposition 3b:
First generation migrants acquire cultural general skills only after a prolongued stay in the mainstream society.

Second generation migrants. While our first generation interviewees clearly indicated their abilities in overcoming cultural barriers with colleagues or business partners from countries they had had no particular exposure to, our data show that *second generation* migrants have even more protracted cultural-general skills.

> As a multicultural, is is much easier when in contact with people from other countries. Of course, knowing the language is always a plus. I am sure that I would be able to reach Latin American clients even better if I knew Spanish or Portuguese. But being the sole multicultural in my team, I could see that I had achieved more in the contact with foreign markets than my colleagues. (second generation, Algeria, 19122015, TR)

> When communicating with other subsidiaries, it makes a difference if you grew up as a multicultural. One is more tolerant if things do not go as planned. For example, when we receive reports from southern countries. They take longer or the reports are not exactly as we need them. According to the German mentality, everything should be perfect. But as a multicultural, I know that habits can differ. (second generation, Kazachstan, 20072016, TR)

Our second generation migrant respondents were very much aware of the abilities their multicultural upbringing offered them, such as flexibility (Chiu & Hong, 2005), tolerance or openness (Benet-Martinez & Haritatos, 2005). And they also realized how valuable these skills could be in a multicultural working context, in particular in situations that were culturally unfamiliar to all concerned parties. This allowed second generation migrants to gain the trust of members from various cultures. As a result, they were able to obtain better outomes.

I also have regular contact with Asians. When I write them, I introduce myself, I tell them what I need, I try not to show any anger if I do not receive the necessary information, and I am thankful for their help. As a result, I noticed that our Asian colleagues send me an answer faster than my German colleagues. I also had to do with controllers from North America. I noticed that US Americans like to do some small talk. And I go along because I know that they feel comfortable with this way of communication. During one telephone conference, my German colleagues began rolling their eyes because we had made small talk for three minutes instead of talking business. I adapt myself but my German colleagues would jump straight into the business part. But this is not how international business works. (second generation, Russia, 29032016, TR)

Even if the notion of shared meaning systems (Hong, 2010) has been previously mostly used in the literature in the context of culture-specific skills, our results seem to suggest that in particular second generation migrants are able to move beyond the specific cultures they grew up in and develop universal meaning systems. This behavioural dexterity (Friedman & Liu, 2009) second generation migrants display goes well beyond the specific.

Furthermore, we noticed that second generation migrants are also highly skilled at identifying behavioral misconceptions of others which could easily evolve into discording work encounters.

I noticed that with such an attitude, the communication would become extremely difficult and in the end, it would escalate into a fight (between Chinese and Germans). When I see this, I intervene and take eveything on an objective level again and try to slow them down in building up such an attitude. (second generation, Mexico, 18092015, TR)

According to the results of our inquiries, second generation migrants very much possess the ability to successfully behave as cultural chameleons. They are able to effectively use these abilities to build a better and stronger connection in various culturally unknown business associates, identify behavioural misconceptions, and improve work outcomes. We thus propose the following:

Proposition 3c:
Second generation migrants have cultural general skills which they employ to improve work outcomes in culturally unknown work situations.

Furthermore, similar to the first generation migrants, we also looked at the defining characteristics of our second generation migrants who aknowledged their culture general skills. We found that by contrast to the first generation, second generation highly qualified migrants were aware of their general skills from early on. To be more specific, our second generation interviewees asserted noticing their universally valid frame swichting abilities long before they entered a multicultural workplace. Based on our intervieews' statements, we conclude that second generation migrants, signifcantly more so than first generation migrants, have a highly effective ingrained set of cultural-general skills which they are able to apply in culturally unfamiliar situations. We thus propose the following:

Proposition 3d:
Second generation migrants possess innate cultural general skills.

3.4.4 Language-general skills of highly qualified migrants

We continued our investigation of highly qualified migrants' general skills and looked into their language general abilities. We thus found some important parallels between culture-general and language-general skills of our *first generation* migrant respondents. To be more specific, we noticed how language-general skills were effectively applied to facilitate cross-national communication.

> On the one side, I know how to "translate" the message from international colleagues to my German colleagues, even if I don't speak their language, so that my German colleagues can understand. And I also know how to convey the message of my German colleagues to our

international colleagues, so that they know what is exactly is expected from them. (first generation, 28092018, Mexico, TR)

I am from India but I can imagine how an Australian would intrepret what a German is saying. Sometimes these are only small communication issues, but I know that when a German says A, the Australian will understand B, because I also used to understand B at the beginning. (first generation, 17052016, India)

According to our results, language-general skills are very similar to culture-general skills in that they are based on a highly developed sense of empathy which became evident when our interviewees encountered and detected communication problems between mainstream and international stakeholders. Based on our findings, we concur with Mughan (2015) who considers language-general skills, similar to culture-general skills, as a collection of diverse abilities such as behavioral adaptability, cross-cultural communication skills and cultural metacognition. Based on our findings, we propose the following:

Proposition 4a:
First generation highly qualified migrants possess language general skills which they employ to improve work outcomes in linguistically unknown work situations.

Despite these similarities, there was one major difference between language-general and culture-general skills: our first generation migrant respondents referred to the former in comparison to the latter with much more scarcity. In these rare instances, we looked closer at potential characteristics which could have played a role in the development of these unique skills. We found that those first generation migrants who conveyed to be able to communicate effectively in culturally and lingistically unfamiliar contexts, had already spent half of their lifetime or at least their career in the mainstream country. It is generally believed that it takes on average five years to develop certain multicultural skills (Benet-Martinez, Leu, Lee & Morris, 2002; Friedman & Liu, 2009). By contrast, our findings seem to suggest that it takes significantly longer to develop language-general skills, which implies that language-general skills are much more complex to develop and apply than culture-general skills. Based on these distinctions, we make the following proposal:

Proposition 4b:
First generation highly qualified migrants need a much more protracted stay in the mainstream society to develop language general skills than culture general skills.

Evaluating our first generation migrant respondends' assertions, we found that they often possess culture-general and much rarer language-general skills which can be useful in culturally and linguistically unexplored situations. These general skills are efficient tools in enhancing communication, creating more harmonious work rapports or improving international business collaborations and this in a much wider set of country-combinations than is the case for culture- and language-specific skills.

Having found this intragenerational distinction pertaining to the development of general skills, we also investigated the particularities of the *second generation* and their language general skills. According to our findings, second generation migrants were frequently able to linguistically facilitate communication also with regard to unfamiliar languages.

> My Hungarian colleague uses a different wording. It is not necessarily false but my German colleagues have difficulties understanding her and they immediately turn to me to perform a sort of translation. (second generation, Turkey, 29042015, TR)

Apparently, second generation migrants have a particular ability to intuitively focus on the core message without getting distracted by improper wording and to employ their empathy to better sense what the speaker wishes to convey. Thus, our findings regarding second generation migrants support Cohen et al. (2015) who argue that language-general skills describe the ability to go beyond the standardized and provide tolerance for divergent utterances or lack of fluency. Moreover, second generation migrants were also skilled at intrepreting messages from a different culture.

> I could always pin point the implicit message better. For example, when a Korean was saying something, I could understand better and

> faster what he was trying to convey. And the same goes for Germans when talking to Asians. Even when I was student I noticed that I have always had a certain advantage here, that I could catch these implicit aspects faster. (second generation, 13052015, Vietnam)

In addition to building bridges with international stakeholders, we found that second generation migrants could also assist with first generation migrants in Germany stemming from various unfamiliar cultures. Our interviewees mentioned that monolingual Germans often had problems to decode messages from first generation migrants with a lower level of German proficiency, leading to problems in building a shared sensemaking and understanding. In these instances, second generation migrants were often much better able to understand such flawed German.

> There are colleagues who are currently integrating in Germany and are still learning the language here. When the right wording does not come to their mind, I can understand what they want to say. For example, we have an Italian colleague who sometimes does not find the right words but I do not have difficulties in understanding him. (second generation, Sri Lanka, 14122015, TR)

It appears that without having internalized a third language, second generation migrants are particularly able to "decode" messages stemming from a linguistically unknown context. Based on these findings, we propose the following:

Proposition 4c:
Second generation highly qualified migrants possess language general skills which they employ to improve work outcomes in linguistically unknown work situations..

Moreover, echoing our findings pertaining to their innate culture general skills, we found that also language general skills were an ability of which second generation migrants became aware from early on. It seems that second generation migrants performed such language brockering activities even during their educational formation period and whenever a situation called for these language general skills, second generation migrants seem to have enabled them automatically. In light of these findings we propose the following:

Proposition 4d:
Second generation highly qualified migrants possess innate language general skills.

Overall, in contrast to the first generation, second generation migrants seem to possess even broader culture- and language-general skills, which they are able to apply more often. They seem also to be more aware of these universally applicable skills at their disposition, having frequently mentioned occasions in which they applied their cultural- and language-general skills from early on in their life, even before the start of their professional career. First generation migrants on the other side, seem to not necessarily have developed these general skills and if so, it took many years of residence in the receiving country to slowly acquire these skills.

Summing up, our findings suggest first generation migrants, in spite of their first-hand culture specific and language specific proficiency, are still dominated by their ethnic cues. This could counterbalance the beneficial effects of their cultural and language bridging activities. Furthermore, they seem to develop culture general and language general skills with the increase of their stay in the mainstream society, with language general skills taking longer to materialize than culture general skills. Second generation migrants on the other hand, seem to have managed to create an equilibrium between their culture specific and language specific abilities. Moreover, their multicultural and multilingual upbringing seem to have conferred them innate culture general and language general skills. We incorporate our findings in a comprehensive framework (Figure 2) of intergenerational as well as intragenerational skill distinctions.

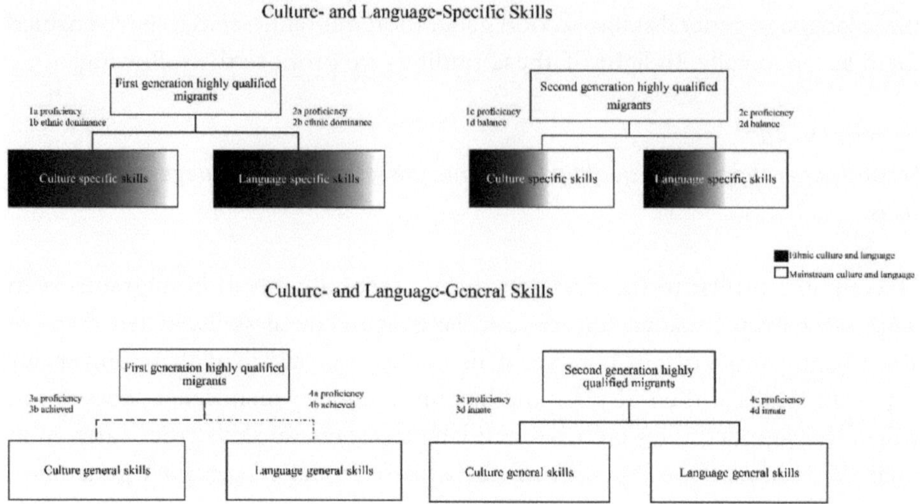

Figure 2. Culture- and language-specific – and general skills of highly qualified migrants

3.5   Discussion

Our study lies at the crossing of two major research streams: (highly qualified) migration, and cross-cultural management. As such, we contribute to a more balanced and comprehensive understanding by differentiating between the first and second generation of (highly qualified) migrants, by displaying the use of migrants' cultural and language skills in multiple organizational contexts, by setting apart the culture skills from the language skills, and by highlighting the difference between specific and general skills. As a result of this extensive and more nuanced overview, our study advances the established beliefs from previous studies.

3.5.1   Theoretical implications

3.5.1.1   *Contributions to migration research*

Previous migration literature has mainly focused on unskilled migrants (e.g. Berry & Bell, 2012; Portes & Fernandes-Kelly, 2008; Simon & Ruhs, 2008). Furthermore, a general belief that migrants are mainly confronted with integration issues (Al Ariss, Koall, Özbilgin & Suutari, 2012) or discrimination (Berry & Sabatier, 2010) persists. Even highly skilled migrants are found to experience underemployment or unemployment in their receiving countries (Al Ariss & Crowley-Henry, 2013). As such, in the migration literature, the positive work experiences of the highly qualified migrant workforce rather go unnoticed and the valuable soft skills they bring with them remain unaddressed (Benson-Rea & Rawlinson, 2003). Through our study, we responded to the call of looking deeper into the experiences of highly qualified migrants (Al Ariss, Cascio & Paauwe, 2014; Guo & Al Ariss, 2015). Based on the considerable research performed in the field of migration, we support the general idea that migrants, regardless of their educational background, face hurdles in their receiving society in looking for accommodation (Berry & Bell, 2012) or when searching for employment (Kaas & Manger, 2011). Nevertheless, we also acknowledge that education influences the adjustment process, and that highly qualified migrants, even though also likely confronted with the usual migration hurdles, adjust faster and better in their receiving society (Yagmur & van der Vijver, 2012).

In our study, we illustrate the importance of looking into the descriptions of individual occurrences to retrieve relevant information from highly qualified migrants who do not seem to be part of the established beliefs about migrant (un)employment. As such, our findings encourage a more comprehensive understanding of the standard migration discourses. Further, we also went beyond the macroeconomic level and focused on a fine-grained analysis at an individual level.

Moreover, we highlighted the importance of the culture and language skills of highly qualified migrants in an organizational context. As mentioned above, the existing migration literature has mainly focused on the downsides of migration from the migrants' point of view. Nevertheless, highly qualified migrants seem to bring in cultural and language skills which could be valuable for an internationally operating company (Benson-Rea & Rawlinson, 2003). Even though we collected individual narratives, we indirectly revealed how international companies in the mainstream economy benefit from the soft skills of highly qualified migrants. As such, we addressed the persistent misapprehensions that companies disregard the qualifications of migrants right from the outset, leading to the well-researched issues of underemployment or even unemployment (Al Ariss & Crowley-Henry, 2013). In fact, we find that our findings surfaced with sufficient clarity in order to make the assessment that in the case of highly qualified migrants, mainstream based companies do recognize their valuable knowledge, skills, abilities, and other characteristics (KSAOs).

We compared the first and second generations of highly qualified migrants in their use of cultural and language skills in a white-collar organizational context, an approach which has seldomly been pursued in such a thorough conceptualization. We considered this contextual avenue to be necessary as the rearing backgrounds of the first generation and the second generation are very much different: our first generation highly qualified migrants grew up in a monocultural and monolingual environment in their ethnic countries and moved to a different country at a later point in their lives (Bee & Boyd, 2002). The second generation, on the other side, typically grew up with two cultures and two languages (Fitzsimmons, 2013). We found it therefore relevant to differentiate between these generations of migrants as the formation of their cultural and language skills is fundamentally different.

By differentiating along the line of educational attainment and generational status, we have been able to provide a more comprehensive illustration of employment experiences of generations of highly qualified migrants.

3.5.1.2 *Contributions to cross-cultural management research*

Additional to our contribution to the migration literature, we furthermore explored a more comprehensive understanding of the multicultural and multilingual skills of migrants. The common interpretive frameworks pertaining to multicultural skills at the organizational level remain mainly theoretical (Backmann et al., 2020). We addressed this gap by empirically looking into not only the skills that highly qualified migrants bring with them or develop them in time, but also at the practical use of these skills in numerous multinational business operations. We therefore empirically developed the ongoing debate on the skills of multiculturals. Also, multiculturals are often believed to undoubtedly be fluent speakers of their respective languages (Furusawa & Brewster, 2015). However, in line with Barner-Rasmussen et al. (2014), we have decided to treat culture and language as two distinct, but nevertheless complementary constructs, thereby gaining a much more comprehensive and thorough perspective on the soft skills of highly qualified migrants. Furthermore, we differentiated between innate and achieved multiculturalism (Martin & Shao, 2016). We consider this distinction to be of significance as the processes through which the first and the second generation migrants become multiculturals are inherently different. On the one side, first generation migrants become immersed with a different culture at a later stage in their lives (Martin & Shao, 2016) and view only one language as their mother tongue (Fitzsimmons, 2013). Therefore, they can be considered as a category of achieved multiculturals (Martin & Shao, 2016). Second generation migrants, on the other side, usually grow up with two languages and tend to have a much more complex form of multicultural identity (Fitzsimmons, 2013; Nguyen & Almadpanah, 2014), thereby developing an innate form of multiculturalism (Martin & Shao, 2016). We contributed to the growing stream of multiculturalism by empirically highlighting the importance of distinguishing between achieved and innate multiculturalism when it comes to their cognitive abilities and the use of these abilities in an organizational context.

We found that first generation migrants, being highly proficient in their ethnic culture and language, are ideal facilitators and decoders when in contact with various ethnic business operations. According to our findings, it seems that the culture specific and language specific skills of the first generation are well acknowledged by their employers. We found that first generation migrants use their specific skills to facilitate a richer information exchange, mediate in impaired sensemaking situations and thus form a shared narrative system, and to circumvent possible conflict situations. Second generation migrants, being immersed in two cultural and linguistic cues from early on, are archetypal cross-cultural bridge makers. Their innate multicultural skills give them a balanced overview on the potential pitfalls of diversity at the workplace, by contrast to first generation migrants who generally consider the ethnic cultural and linguistic repertoire as dominant due to their late immersion in a new country context. Nevertheless, second generation migrants occasionally use their specific skills in an informal manner. This concurs with Barner-Rasmussen et al. (2014) and Blazejewski (2012) that effective cross-cultural bridge makers are not necessarily only in leadership positions and that other intrinsic motivational factors might play a role when individuals actively use their cross-cultural skills at work.

We also investigated the general skills of first and second generation highly qualified migrants. If the culture and language specific skills are quite apparent to pinpoint, the general skills have proven to be somewhat complex to define, not to mention to empirically test. Through the rich descriptions of our interviewees, we gathered milestones in their development and use of culture general and language general skills. We have found that first generation migrants are able to widen their skills to culture general and language general abilities and use them to improve cross-cultural communication and understanding. It is generally believed that it takes a minimum of five years to develop certain multicultural skills (Benet-Martinezet al., 2002; Friedman & Liu, 2009). First generation migrants need at least twice as long to build up the culture general and language general skills. To be more specific, we found that not only the development of these universal skills requires a prolongued residence in the mainstream society, but also that language general skills need even more time to unfold than culture general skills. As such, we found that the ability of first generation migrants to withdraw valuable lessons from their international mobility and develop these ubiquitous skills is subject to the time spent in the mainstream country. Furthermore, by contrast to our first generation respondents, the second generation seems to consider these wide-ranging skills as a matter of implicitness and mentioned having used their general skills from early on, i.e. before the start of their professional careers. In a multinational work context, second generation respondents asserted having used their skills in enhancing international business collaboration and reaching more positive outcomes, improving communication stemming from a culturally unfamiliar context, or creating a shared sense-making where the use of the corporate language failed to do so. Thus, we find that generational status does play a role in the development of culture general and language general skills.

Even though communication is highly intertwined with the cultural framework (Zhong & Chin, 2015), we additionally viewed the cultural and language skills separately in order to reveal the distinctions between cross-cultural organizational processes attached to each type of skill. The existing conceptualizations have considered the language skills of multiculturals as embedded in the cultural skills (Luna , Ringberg & Peracchio, 2008; Ringberg, Luna, Reihlen & Peracchio 2010). Up until recently, language has often been a neglected subject in the international business research (Tietze, Piekkari & Brannen, 2014). By separating between these concepts in our data, we responded to the request to view language separately (Welch & Welch, 2008).

Multiculturals' skills have been found to be valuable in the context of HQ-subsidiary relations (Barner-Rasmussen et al., 2014), in the management of

MNTs (Hong, 2010), when making strategical decisions or internationally complex ethical decisions (Fitzsimmons et al., 2011). Due to the qualitative nature of our study, we were open in our data gathering to any potential occurrences in which highly qualified migrants used their cultural and language skills. We therefore found that they used their skills in various business contexts, ranging from HQ-subsidiary relations, to international clients or in-site workplace interaction with first generation migrants. Therefore, we based our study on the established beliefs of previous research, but we also contributed to a more balanced and comprehensive understanding of the use of multiculturals' skills, by going beyond the common interpretive frames.

3.5.2 Managerial implications

Taking the white-collar positions and the use of our interviewee's skills in consideration, we contrast with the persistent beliefs that migrants are generally disadvantaged in their job search (Kaas & Manger, 2011), not to mention in their possibility of using their cultural and language skills at work. We generally agree with the findings from previous research about the employment disadvantages of migrants but we also believe, in accordance with our findings, that highly qualified migrants are also given the possibility to make fulfilling career choices or to use their cultural and language skills in an organizational context.

Migrants' skills, as a category of multiculturals, are valuable, rare, and hard to imitate intangible assets which could be used by companies to remain successful and competitive at an international level (Brannen & Thomas, 2010). These skills also have to be organizationally embedded so that migrants use them in an optimal manner for the company (Thomas, 2016; Zanoni, Janssens, Benschop & Nkomo, 2010). By contrast to the first generation, second generation migrants are ideally immersed in two cultures and languages. As such, they could prove to be prototypical cross-cultural bridge makers. As we found that second generation migrants often use their skills informally or when circumstances dictated, we suggest that managers take the background and motivation of second generation highly qualified employees into account when assigning tasks with an international business focus. This could lead to a better overlap between company needs and migrant skills.

We additionally went beyond the classical frameworks that multiculturals are valuable in managing MNTs (Hong, 2010), when making strategic choices (Fitzsimmons et al., 2011), or when spanning the organization's boundaries (Barner-Rasmussen et al., 2014). Pertaining to our results, second generation migrants, for example, use their skills in creating a more harmonious relation with international clients. These activities might be considered rather modest by contrast to the management of whole MNTs, but they do contribute to positive results in daily international operations. With our findings, we managed to broaden the understanding of multicultural migrant skills' implementation and effects.

3.5.3 Limitations and suggestions for future research

We fully acknowledge that our study has the following limitations: although we interviewed highly qualified migrants from a wide array of positions from multiple industries and functional positions, the country context was kept constant, i.e. Germany. Our decision to pursue such a methodological line was to keep the mainstream culture, and institutional and economic framework consistent. Furthermore, most of the semi-structured interviews were conducted in the southern part of Germany, a region known to be economically prosperous, with a low level of unemployment and a high level of shortage of skilled labour. Although migration usually takes place from less developed regions to developed regions (Iredale, 2001), we acknowledge that a study performed in another context, i.e. with lower economic development and high level of unemployment, would potentially render different results.

The use of cultural and language skills is also dependant on the job position one holds and the intrinsic motivation to do so. We have had interviewees from both categories of migrants, i.e. first and second generation who, although they performed cross-cultural activities, did not express the desire to go further in such a cross-cultural bridge making direction, at least career wise. Our results are therefore also influenced by the intrinsic motivation of our respondents to use their skills. Another additional aspect which might play a role is the functional position they held in the company. For certain job categories, such as engineers, these soft skills are considered less valuable than in positions in which communication skills are much more important, i.e. sales or marketing, an aspect which was also mentioned by our interviewees. We encourage future researchers to additionally look into the functional area of multicultural migrants and the propensity to use their cultural and language skills.

Furthermore, since defining culture general and language general skills is a rather complex task, their investigation is much more the challenging. We have found generational status, or time spent in the mainstream society, to be a relevant factor in the development of such skills, but we are also aware that there are other potential circumstances which can lead to the development of these culture general and language general skills. Future research could focus on advancing the literature in this respect even further and take other aspects in consideration, such as the Big Five personality traits.

Regarding the development of multicultural skills of first generation migrants, we acknowledge that reason to migrate could influence the willingness to adapt, in spite of the high educational level. Being confronted with a push or pull factor in the decision to migrate can potentially motivate and at the same time demotivate an individual to adapt in a given receiving country and become proficient in the mainstream culture and language. Hence, even if assimilation takes place, the duration of such processes might be dependent on the reason to leave the homeland.

3.6 Conclusion

Our study responds to frequent calls of investigating in more detail the particular skills and working experiences of highly qualified migrants. Based on rich qualitative interview data, we add to previous literature, demonstrating that highly skilled migrants possess particular cultural and language skills that can be highly useful for their employing organizations. Having said this, our study clearly shows that in order to properly evaluate those cultural and language skills, it is highly useful to differentiate between first and second generation migrants, as their skill sets differentiate in important ways. More specifically, we established that first generation highly qualified migrants do possess proficient culture and language specific skills, which they effectively implement to improve multinational work outcomes. Nevertheless, their ethnic dominance puts a strain on their own work outcomes in the mainstream context. Second generation migrants on the other hand have balanced culture and language specific skills. Furthermore, first generation migrants need considerably more time to develop culture general and language general skills, compared to second generation migrants who naturally develop these skills as they grow up. In doing so, our study offers new paths for more nuanced investigations pertaining to the valuable soft skills highly qualified migrants bring in.

3.7 References

Al Ariss, A., & Crowley-Henry, M. (2013). Self-initiated expatriation and migration in the management literature: Present theorizations and future research directions. *Career Development International, 18*(1), 78-96.

Al Ariss, A., Cascio, W. F., & Paauwe, J. (2014). Talent management: Current theories and future research directions. *Journal of World Business, 49*(2), 173-179.

Al Ariss, A., Koall, I., Ozbilgin, M., Suutari, V., & Özbilgin, M. (2012). Careers of skilled migrants: towards a theoretical and methodological expansion. *Journal of Management Development. 31*(2), 92-101

Amaram, D. I. (2007). Cultural diversity: Implications for workplace management. *Journal of Diversity Management (JDM), 2*(4), 1-6.

Backmann, J., Kanitz, R., Tian, A. W., Hoffmann, P., & Hoegl, M. (2020). Cultural gap bridging in multinational teams. *Journal of International Business Studies*, 1-29.

Bakker, W., Van Der Zee, K., & Van Oudenhoven, J. P. (2006). Personality and Dutch emigrants' reactions to acculturation strategies. *Journal of Applied Social Psychology, 36*(12), 2864-2891.

Barner-Rasmussen, W. (2015). What do bicultural-bilinguals do in multinational corporations. In N. Holden, S. Michailova & S. Tietze (Eds). *The Routledge companion to cross-cultural management*: 142-150. London and New York: Routledge.

Barner-Rasmussen, W., Ehrnrooth, M., Koveshnikov, A., & Mäkelä, K. (2008). Kingpins of the multinational: On the characteristics and roles of boundary spanners in multinational corporations. In *34th EIBA Conference, Tallinn* (pp. 11-13).

Barner-Rasmussen, W., Ehrnrooth, M., Koveshnikov, A., & Mäkelä, K. (2014). Cultural and language skills as resources for boundary spanning within the MNC. *Journal of International Business Studies, 45*(7), 886-905.

Bee, H., & Boyd, D. (2002). Social and personality development in middle adulthood. *Lifespan development*, 429-455.

Beechler, S., Søndergaard, M., Miller, E. L., & Bird, A. (2004). Boundary spanning. In H. Lane, M. Maznevski, M.E. Mendenhall, J.Mcnett (Eds), *The Blackwell handbook of global management: A guide to managing complexity*, 121-133, Oxford: Blackwell Publishing.

Beiser. M., Barwick, C., Berry, J.W., da Costa. G., Fantino, A., Ganesan. S., Lee. C., Milne. W. Naidoo., J. Prince, R., Tousignant. M., & Vela, E. (1988). *Mental health issues affecting immigrants and refugees*. Ottawa: Health and Welfare Canada.

Bell, E., & Bryman, A. (2007). The ethics of management research: an exploratory content analysis. *British Journal of Management*, *18*(1), 63-77.

Bell, M. P., & Harrison, D. A. (1996). Using intra-national diversity for international assignments: A model of bicultural competence and expatriate adjustment. *Human Resource Management Review*, *6*(1), 47-74.

Benet-Martínez, V., & Haritatos, J. (2005). Bicultural identity integration (BII): Components and psychosocial antecedents. *Journal of Personality*, *73*(4), 1015-1050.

Benet-Martínez, V., Lee, F., & Leu, J. (2006). Biculturalism and cognitive complexity: Expertise in cultural representations. *Journal of Cross-Cultural Psychology*, *37*(4), 386-407.

Benet-Martínez, V., Leu, J., Lee, F., & Morris, M. W. (2002). Negotiating biculturalism: Cultural frame switching in biculturals with oppositional versus compatible cultural identities. *Journal of Cross-cultural psychology*, *33*(5), 492-516.

Benson-Rea, M., & Rawlinson, S. (2003). Highly skilled and business migrants: Information processes and settlement outcomes. *International Migration*, *41*(2), 59-79.

Berg, M. L., & Eckstein, S. (2009). Introduction: Reimagining migrant generations. *Diaspora: A Journal of Transnational Studies*, *18*(1), 1-23.

Berry, D. P., & Bell, M. P. (2012). 'Expatriates': gender, race and class distinctions in international management. *Gender, Work & Organization*, *19*(1), 10-28.

Berry, J. W. (1997). Immigration, acculturation, and adaptation. *Applied Psychology*, *46*(1), 5-34.

Berry, J. W., & Sabatier, C. (2010). Acculturation, discrimination, and adaptation among second generation immigrant youth in Montreal and Paris. *International Journal of Intercultural Relations, 34*(3), 191-207.

Bierbrauer, G., & Klinger, E. W. (2005). The influence of conflict context characteristics on conflict regulation preferences of immigrants. *Journal of Cross-Cultural Psychology, 36*(3), 340-354.

Blazejewski, S. 2012. Betwixt or beyond the lines of conflict? Biculturalism as situated identity in multinational corporations. *Critical Perspectives on International Business, 8*(2), 111–135

Blazejewski, S., & Becker-Ritterspach, F. (2011). *Conflict in headquarters-subsidiary relations: a critical literature review and new directions* (pp. 139-190). Cambridge: Cambridge University Press.

Brannen, M. Y., & Thomas, D. C. (2010). Bicultural individuals in organizations: Implications and opportunity. *International Journal of Cross-Cultural Management, 10*(1), 5-16.

Brannen, M. Y., Garcia, D., & Thomas, D. C. (2009). Biculturals as natural bridges for intercultural communication and collaboration. In *Proceedings of the 2009 international Workshop on Intercultural Collaboration* (pp. 207-210).

Brinkmann, S., & Kvale, S. (2015). Conducting an interview. *Interviews. Learning the craft of qualitative research Interviewing*, 149-166.

Carlile, P. R. (2004). Transferring, translating, and transforming: An integrative framework for managing knowledge across boundaries. *Organization Science, 15*(5), 555-568.

Chiu, C. Y., & Hong, Y. Y. (2005). Cultural Competence: Dynamic Processes. In: Elliot A. & Dweck C.S.(Eds.), 1-45, *Handbook of Competence and Motivation*. New York: Guilford.

Cohen, L., Kassis-Henderson, J., & Lecomte, P. (2015). Language diversity in management education. In N. Holden, S. Michailova & S. Tietze (Eds). *The Routledge companion to cross-cultural management*, 151. London and New York: Routledge

Crul, M., & Doomernik, J. (2003). The Turkish and Moroccan Second Generation in the Netherlands: Divergent Trends between and Polarization within the Two Groups. *International Migration Review, 37*(4), 1039-1064.

Daft, R. L., & Lewin, A. Y. (1993). Where are the theories for the" new" organizational forms? An editorial essay. *Organization Science*, i-vi.

Dau, L. A. (2016). Biculturalism, team performance, and cultural-faultline bridges. *Journal of International Management, 22*(1), 48-62.

Denzin, N. K. (2017). *The research act: A theoretical introduction to sociological methods.* New York: Routledge.

Edmondson, A. C., & McManus, S. E. (2007). Methodological fit in management field research. *Academy of Management Review, 32*(4), 1246-1264.

Eisenhardt, K. M. (1989). Agency theory: An assessment and review. *Academy of Management Review, 14*(1), 57-74.

Eisenhardt, K. M., & Graebner, M. E. (2007). Theory building from cases: Opportunities and challenges. *Academy of Management Journal, 50*(1), 25-32.

Fiedler, S. (2010). The English-as-a-lingua-franca approach: Linguistic fair play? *Language Problems and Language Planning, 34*(3), 201-221.

Fitzsimmons, S. R. (2013). Multicultural employees: A framework for understanding how they contribute to organizations. *Academy of Management Review, 38*(4), 525-549.

Fitzsimmons, S.R., Miska, C. & Stahl, G.K. (2011). Multicultural employees: Global business' untapped resource. *Organizational Dynamics, 40*(3), 199-206.

Friedman, R., & Liu, W. (2009). Biculturalism in Management. In R.S. Wyer, C. Chiu & Y. Hong (Eds). *Understanding culture: Theory, research, and application,* 333 - 350. New York: Taylor and Francis.

Fujio, M. (2004). Silence during intercultural communication: A case study. *Corporate Communications: An International Journal, 9*(4), 331-339.

Furusawa, M., & Brewster, C. (2015). The bi-cultural option for global talent management: The Japanese/Brazilian Nikkeijin example. *Journal of World Business, 50*(1), 133-143.

Gioia, D. A., Corley, K. G., & Hamilton, A. L. (2013). Seeking qualitative rigor in inductive research: Notes on the Gioia methodology. *Organizational Research Methods, 16*(1), 15-31.

Glaser, B., Strauss, A., (1967). The Discovery of Grounded Theory. Aldine Publishing Company, Hawthorne, New York

Gong, L. (2007). Ethnic identity and identification with the majority group: Relations with national identity and self-esteem. *International Journal of Intercultural Relations, 31*(4), 503-523.

Guo, C., & Al Ariss, A. (2015). Human resource management of international migrants: current theories and future research. *International Journal of Human Resource Management, 26*(10), 1287-1297.

Hajro, A., & Pudelko, M. (2010). An analysis of core-competences of successful multinational team leaders. *International Journal of Cross-Cultural Management, 10*(2), 175-194.

Hajro, A., Zilinskaite, M., & Stahl, G. (2017). Acculturation of highly-qualified migrants: individual coping strategies and climate for inclusion. In *Academy of Management Proceedings* (Vol. 2017, No. 1, p. 13666). Briarcliff Manor, NY 10510: Academy of Management.

Harzing, A. W., & Maznevski, M. (2002). The interaction between language and culture: A test of the cultural accommodation hypothesis in seven countries. *Language and Intercultural Communication, 2*(2), 120-139.

Harzing, A. W., & Pudelko, M. (2013). Language competencies, policies and practices in multinational corporations: A comprehensive review and comparison of Anglophone, Asian, Continental European and Nordic MNCs. *Journal of World Business, 48*(1), 87-97.

Harzing, A. W., Köster, K., & Magner, U. (2011). Babel in business: The language barrier and its solutions in the HQ-subsidiary relationship. *Journal of World Business, 46*(3), 279-287.

Heath, A. F., Rothon, C., & Kilpi, E. (2008). The second generation in Western Europe: Education, unemployment, and occupational attainment. *Annual Review in Sociology, 34*, 211-235.

Hofhuis, J., van Der Zee, K. I., & Otten, S. (2012). Social Identity Patterns in Culturally Diverse Organizations: The Role of Diversity Climate 1. *Journal of Applied Social Psychology, 42*(4), 964-989.

Hong, H. J. (2010). Bicultural competence and its impact on team effectiveness. *International Journal of Cross Cultural Management, 10*(1), 93-120.

Hong, H. J., & Doz, Y. (2013). L'Oreal masters multiculturalism. *Harvard Business Review, 91*(6), 114-118.

Hong, H. J., & Minbaeva, D. B. (2017). Multiculturals as Strategic Human Capital Resources in Multinational Enterprises. In *Academy of Management Proceedings* (Vol. 2017, No. 1, p. 15896). Briarcliff Manor, NY 10510: Academy of Management.

Hutzschenreuter, T., & Voll, J. C. (2008). Performance effects of "added cultural distance" in the path of international expansion: The case of German multinational enterprises. *Journal of International Business Studies, 39*(1), 53-70.

Iredale, R. (2001). The migration of professionals: theories and typologies. *International Migration, 39*(5), 7-26.

Kaas, L., & Manger, C. (2011). Ethnic discrimination in Germany's labour market: a field experiment. *German Economic Review, 13*(1), 1-20.

Kane, A. A., & Levina, N. (2017). 'Am I still one of them?': Bicultural immigrant managers navigating social identity threats when spanning global boundaries. *Journal of Management Studies, 54*(4), 540-577.

Kassis-Henderson, J., Cohen, L., & McCulloch, R. (2018). Boundary crossing and reflexivity: Navigating the complexity of cultural and linguistic identity. *Business and Professional Communication Quarterly, 81*(3), 304-327.

Kofman, E., & Raghuram, P. (2006). Gender and global labour migrations: Incorporating skilled workers. *Antipode, 38*(2), 282-303.

Kostova, T., & Roth, K. (2003). Social capital in multinational corporations and a micro-macro model of its formation. *Academy of management review, 28*(2), 297-317.

LaFromboise, T., Coleman, H. L., & Gerton, J. (1993). Psychological impact of biculturalism: Evidence and theory. *Psychological Bulletin, 114*(3), 395.

Langley, A. (1999). Strategies for theorizing from process data. *Academy of Management Review, 24*(4), 691-710.

Lee, T. W. (1999). *Using qualitative methods in organizational research.* Thousand Oaks: Sage.

Levitt, P. (2009). Roots and routes: Understanding the lives of the second generation transnationally. *Journal of Ethnic and Migration Studies, 35*(7), 1225-1242.

Locke, K. (2001). *Grounded theory in management research.* Thousand Oaks, CA: Sage Publications.

Lücke, G., Kostova, T., & Roth, K. (2014). Multiculturalism from a cognitive perspective: Patterns and implications. *Journal of International Business Studies, 45*(2), 169-190.

Lücke, G., & Roth, K. (2008). *An embeddedness view of biculturalism.* Working Paper D-08-07, South Carolina CIBER Working Paper Series.

Luna, D., Ringberg, T., & Peracchio, L. A. (2008). One individual, two identities: Frame switching among biculturals. *Journal of Consumer Research, 35*(2), 279-293.

Luo, Y., & Shenkar, O. (2006). The multinational corporation as a multilingual community: Language and organization in a global context. *Journal of International Business Studies, 37*(3), 321-339.

Marschan-Piekkari, R., Welch, D., & Welch, L. (1999). In the shadow: The impact of language on structure, power and communication in the multinational. *International Business Review, 8*(4), 421-440.

Martin, L., & Shao, B. (2016). Early immersive culture mixing: The key to understanding cognitive and identity differences among multiculturals. *Journal of Cross-Cultural Psychology, 47*(10), 1409-1429.

Mattoo, A., Neagu, I. C., & Ozden, C. (2008). Brain waste? Educated immigrants in the US labor market. *Journal of Development Economics, 87*, 255-269.

Mazur, B. (2010). Cultural diversity in organisational theory and practice. *Journal of intercultural management, 2*(2), 5-15.

Merton, R. K. (1968). *Social theory and social structure*. New York: The Free Press

Miles, M. B., & Huberman, A. M. (1994). *Qualitative data analysis: An expanded sourcebook*. New York: Sage.

Milliken, F. J., & Martins, L. L. (1996). Searching for common threads: Understanding the multiple effects of diversity in organizational groups. *Academy of Management Review, 21*(2), 402-433.

Molinsky, A. (2007). Cross-cultural code-switching: The psychological challenges of adapting behavior in foreign cultural interactions. *Academy of Management Review, 32*(2), 622-640.

Moore, A. M., & Barker, G. G. (2012). Confused or multicultural: Third culture individuals' cultural identity. *International Journal of Intercultural Relations, 36*(4), 553-562.

Mughan, T. (2015). Introduction: language and languages: moving from the periphery to the core. In N. Holden, S. Michailova & S. Tietze (Eds). *The Routledge companion to cross-cultural management*, 129-134. London and New York: Routledge.

Myers, M. D. (2008). *Qualitative research in business and management*. Thousand Oaks, CA: Sage.

Nahapiet, J., & Ghoshal, S. (1998). Social capital, intellectual capital, and the organizational advantage. *Academy of Management Review, 23*(2), 242-266.

Nguyen, A. M. D., & Ahmadpanah, S. S. (2014). The interplay between bicultural blending and dual language acquisition. *Journal of Cross-Cultural Psychology*, *45*(8), 1215-1220.

Nguyen, A. M. D., & Benet-Martínez, V. (2007). Biculturalism unpacked: Components, measurement, individual differences, and outcomes. *Social and Personality Psychology Compass*, *1*(1), 101-114.

Nguyen, A. M. D., & Benet-Martínez, V. (2013). Biculturalism and adjustment: A meta-analysis. *Journal of Cross-Cultural Psychology*, *44*(1), 122-159.

OECD (2017). *G20 global displacement and migration report trends report*. Available online: https://www.oecd.org/g20/topics/employment-and-social-policy/G20-OECD-migration.pdf [Accessed on 15 October 2018]

Pelled, L. H., Eisenhardt, K. M., & Xin, K. R. (1999). Exploring the black box: An analysis of work group diversity, conflict and performance. *Administrative Science Quarterly*, *44*(1), 1-28.

Polek, E., van Oudenhoven, J. P., & ten Berge, J. M. (2008). Attachment styles and demographic factors as predictors of sociocultural and psychological adjustment of Eastern European immigrants in the Netherlands. *International Journal of Psychology*, *43*(5), 919-928.

Portes, A., & Fernández-Kelly, P. (2008). No margin for error: Educational and occupational achievement among disadvantaged children of immigrants. *The Annals of the American Academy of Political and Social Science*, *620*(1), 12-36.

Pratt, M. G. (2009). From the editors: For the lack of a boilerplate: Tips on writing up (and reviewing) qualitative research. *Academy of Management Journal*, *52*(5), 856-862

Recchi , E. and Nebe , T. (2003) Migration and Political Identity in the European Union: Research Issues and Theoretical Premises , Florence : CIUSPO , *PIONEUR Working Paper No. 1* Ringberg, T. V., Luna, D., Reihlen, M., & Peracchio, L. A. (2010). Bicultural-bilinguals: The effect of cultural frame switching on translation equivalence. *International Journal of Cross-Cultural Management*, *10*(1), 77-92.

Siggelkow, N. (2007). Persuasion with case studies. *Academy of Management Journal*, *50*(1), 20-24.

Simon, B., & Ruhs, D. (2008). Identity and politicization among Turkish migrants in Germany: the role of dual identification. *Journal of Personality and Social Psychology*, *95*(6), 1354.

Sinkovics, R. R., Penz, E., & Ghauri, P. N. (2008). Enhancing the trustworthiness of qualitative research in international business. *Management International Review, 48*(6), 689-714.

Squires, A. (2009). Methodological challenges in cross-language qualitative research: a research review. *International Journal of Nursing Studies, 46*(2), 277-287.

Stadler, S. A. (2017). Which competence? A comparative analysis of culture-specific vs. culture-generic intercultural competence development. *Advances in Economics and Business, 5*, 448-455.

Statistisches Bundesamt – Destatis. (2020). *Migration und Integration.* Available online: https://www.destatis.de/DE/Themen/Gesellschaft-Umwelt/Bevoelkerung/Migration-Integration/_inhalt.html. [Accessed 22 April 2021]

Steyaert, C., Ostendorp, A., & Gaibrois, C. (2011). Multilingual organizations as 'linguascapes': Negotiating the position of English through discursive practices. *Journal of World Business, 46*(3), 270-278.

Strauss, A., & Corbin, J. (1998). *Basics of qualitative research: Techniques and procedures for developing grounded theory*, 2nd ed. Thousand Oaks: Sage.

Suddaby, R. (2006). From the editors: What grounded theory is not. *Academy of Management Journal, 49*(4), 633-642

Tenzer, H., & Pudelko, M. (2017). The influence of language differences on power dynamics in multinational teams. *Journal of World Business, 52*(1), 45-61.

Thomas, D. (2016). *The multicultural mind: Unleashing the hidden force for innovation in your organization.* Oakland: Berrett-Koehler Publishers.

Thomas, D. C., Liao, Y., Aycan, Z., Cerdin, J. L., Pekerti, A. A., Ravlin, E. C., Stahl, G.K., Lazarova, M.B., Fock, H., Arli, D., Moeller, M., Okimoto, T.G., van de Vijver, F. (2015). Cultural intelligence: A theory-based, short form measure. *Journal of International Business Studies, 46*(9), 1099-1118.

Thomson, M., & Crul, M. (2007). The second generation in Europe and the United States: How is the transatlantic debate relevant for further research on the European second generation? *Journal of Ethnic and Migration Studies, 33*(7), 1025-1041.

Tietze, S., Piekkari, R., & Brannen, M. Y. (2014). From standardisation to localisation: developing a language-sensitive approach to IHRM. In *The*

Routledge Companion to International Human Resource Management (pp. 508-521). Routledge.

Van Der Zee, K. I., & Van Oudenhoven, J. P. (2000). The Multicultural Personality Questionnaire: A multidimensional instrument of multicultural effectiveness. *European Journal of Personality, 14*(4), 291-309.

Van Laer, K., & Janssens, M. (2011). Ethnic minority professionals' experiences with subtle discrimination in the workplace. *Human Relations, 64*(9), 1203-1227.

Vora, D., Martin, L., Fitzsimmons, S. R., Pekerti, A. A., Lakshman, C., & Raheem, S. (2019). Multiculturalism within individuals: A review, critique, and agenda for future research. *Journal of International Business Studies, 50*(4), 499-524.

Weiss, R. S. (1994). *Learning from strangers*. New York. Free Press

Welch, D. E., & Welch, L. S. (2008). The importance of language in international knowledge transfer. *Management International Review, 48*(3), 339-360.

Wierzbicka, A. (2003). *Cross-cultural Pragmatics: The Semantics of Human Interaction* (Vol. 53). Walter de Gruyter.

Witzel, A. (2000). The problem-centered interview. Forum: Qualitative Social Research, 1(1), Available online: http://www.qualitative-research.net/index.php/fqs/article/view/1132/2521, accessed 15 September 2018.

Worbs, S. (2003). The second generation in Germany: between school and labor market. *International Migration Review, 37*(4), 1011-1038.

Yağmur, K., & van de Vijver, F. J. (2012). Acculturation and language orientations of Turkish immigrants in Australia, France, Germany, and the Netherlands. *Journal of Cross-Cultural Psychology, 43*(7), 1110-1130.

Yanaprasart, P. (2015). Making an asset of multilingual human resources in organizations. In N. Holden, S. Michailova & S. Tietze (Eds). *The Routledge companion to cross-cultural management*, 112. London and New York: Routledge.

Yeung, H. W. C. (1995). Qualitative personal interviews in international business research: some lessons from a study of Hong Kong transnational corporations. *International Business Review, 4*(3), 313-339.

Zanoni, P., Janssens, M., Benschop, Y., & Nkomo, S. (2010). Guest editorial: Unpacking diversity, grasping inequality: Rethinking difference through critical perspectives. *Organization, 17*(1), 9-29.

Zhong, W., & Chin, T. 2015. The role of translation in cross-cultural knowledge transfer within a MNE's business networks: a 3D-hierarchical model in China. *Chinese Management Studies*, 9(4), 589-610.

4. The impact of cultural identity on cross-cultural and cross-lingual bridging skills of highly qualified migrants

Abstract

This inductive study explores on the basis of 130 interviews (a) the cultural identity of highly qualified migrants and (b) the impact of different forms of migrants' cultural identity on their cross-cultural and cross-lingual bridging skills. With this research agenda in mind, we specifically tease out the differences between first and second generation highly qualified migrants. We find that identity changes can take place within generations, by contrast to the common belief, that cultural identities change between generations of migrants. We thus establish two sub-groups for the first generation of migrants: those with an ethnic identity *("anchored migrants")* and those with a split identity *("torn migrants")*; similarly, we find two sub-groups for the second generation of migrants: those with a plural identity *("adaptive migrants")* and those with a mainstream identity *("reborn migrants")*. Pertaining to their bridging skills, we ascertain that *anchored migrants, torn migrants,* and *reborn migrants* have limited cultural and language bridging skills. By contrast, *adaptive migrants* have both proficient cultural and language bridging skills. Thus, they are ideal bridging agents due to their dual cultural and language embeddedness. Our study demonstrates the need for a more nuanced understanding of migrant identity processes, in particular regarding generational differences, upon investigating migrants' bridging skills.

4.1 Introduction

Globalization is a multi-facetted phenomenon, impacting the demographic composition of entire nations via migration but also of multinational corporations (MNCs). At a societal level, the adaptation and settlement of new cultural groups (Grzymala-Kazlowska & Phillimore, 2018) and the subsequent challenges have often been a significant part in the migrant integration debate (Korteweg, 2017). However, the integration of globalization driven diversity is relevant not only for receiving societies (Gregurović & Županić-Iljić, 2018), but also for MNCs, given their highly diverse workforce in terms of cultures and languages. For example, the cultural diversity of internationally operating companies has led to a plethora of business challenges (Pelled, Eisenhardt & Xin, 1999; Stahl & Tung, 2015) such as hampering organizational learning (Barkema, Bell & Pennings, 1996). Language diversity can also have an adverse impact on the functioning and outcomes of multinational operations (Kostova & Roth, 2003), such as team building issues or loss of trust (Henderson, 2005). In order to facilitate business operations taking place in a culturally and linguistically diverse environment, employees with particular cross-cultural and cross-lingual bridging skills are believed to be of particular relevance (Sekiguchi, 2016).

Bridge individuals have been defined as possessing valuable cultural and language skills which allow them to connect different organizational members who are separated by cultural and language differences (Sekiguchi, 2016). To be more specific, bridge individuals are able to understand and span cultural faultlines within multinational organizations (Brannen, Garcia & Thomas, 2009). By engaging in such bridging activities, they facilitate cross-cultural coordination and communication or even create synergies between culturally distinct organizational members (Dau, 2016). As a result, the cultural bridging activities they undertake reduces the "us vs them" thinking which could have detrimental effects on the functioning of international business operations (Fitzsimmons, Miska & Stahl, 2011). Similar to their cross-cultural bridging activities, bridge individuals are also able to engage in linguistic spanning activities (Barner-Rasmussen, 2015; Barner-Rasmussen, Ehrnrooth, Koveshnikov & Mäkelä, 2008). Their high linguistic proficiency in multiple languages enables them the ability to act as translators between international organizational members (Harzing, Köster & Magner, 2011). In line with Barner-Rasmussen, Ehrnrooth, Koveshnikov & Mäkelä (2014:890), we view cultural and language skills as "conceptually distinct, but related and complementary". For this reason, we look into both cultural and language skills that bridge individuals employ in a multinational working context.

Research on bridge individuals has primarily focused on expatriates, thus leaving the cross-cultural and language skills of highly skilled migrants largely unrecognized (Benson-Rea & Rawlinson, 2003). Migrants possess an in-depth cultural and language understanding of their respective ethnic country (or country-of-origin) which they can employ in business operations with ethnic business partners (Kane & Levina, 2017). Furthermore, due to profound adaptation processes which they undergo in their respective receiving country (or mainstream country), they also develop a cultural and language expertise in the receiving country's context. Initial research has further suggested the educational background of migrants to be of relevance for the formation of bridging skills, as higher educational levels have been found to positively impact migrants' adaptation to their receiving countries (Berry, 1997; Polek, van Oudenhoven & ten Berge, 2008). Furthermore, in spite of the generally acknowledged value of highly qualified migrants for their organizations, this group remains rather under-researched from a management perspective (Al Ariss, Cascio, Paauwe, 2014). To be more specific, management research on skilled migrants focuses on their experiences until their reach suitable employment, rarely exploring post-employment experiences (Tharenou & Kulik, 2020). As a result, the use of their cultural and language skills and subsequent bridging activities they undertake remain rather under-explored from a management perspective.

Moreover, migration research has predominantly investigated migration from a macro-economic standpoint (Al Ariss & Syed, 2011), by addressing phenomena such as brain drain (Baruch, Budhwar & Khatri, 2007), immigration policies (Guo & Al Ariss, 2015) or the educational shortfalls of migrants (Crul & Doomernik, 2003). As a result, the individual level of (highly skilled) migrants, such as their career development and their particular skills have remained a largely unaddressed topic (Al Ariss, 2010; Al Ariss, Koall, Özbilgin & Suutari, 2012).

Apart from the educational distinction, we argue that also a generational differentiation is of relevance: *first generation migrants* were born in a different national context from the receiving country (Gong, 2007) and their identity tends to remain strongly rooted in their ethnic heritage (Fitzsimmons, 2013); by contrast, *second generation migrants* are the offspring of the first generation (Worbs, 2003) and tend to develop plural forms of identity, as they usually have an attachment towards both the ethnic culture of their parents and the mainstream culture into which they were born (Fitzsimmons, 2013). Despite the relevance of cultural identity for bridging skills (Sekiguchi, 2016) and potentially striking differences in cultural identity formation between first and second generation migrants, the generational distinction in migrants' cultural and language skills has rarely been comprehensively investigated (Martin & Shao, 2016). We consider this to be a shortcoming of conceptual relevance and simultaneously an issue of practical significance which therefore merits exploration. Based on these considerations, we focused on the following research question: *how do the first and the second generation of highly qualified migrants differ in the impact of their cultural identity on their cross-cultural and cross-lingual bridging skills?*

Our research undertaking is thus multifaceted as we intend to explore: a nuanced and differentiated understanding of migrants' cultural identity; the impact of different forms of migrants' cultural identity on their bridging skills; the differentiation between cross-cultural and cross-lingual bridging skills; the focus on highly skilled migrants; and the differentiation between first and second generation migrants. Due to the complexity of these interrelated aspects, we considered an explorative and inductive approach best suited for our research purposes (Pratt, 2009).

To reduce contextual complexity, we decided to conduct our study in only one migrant receiving country, namely Germany. At around 26 per cent population with a migration background (Destatis, 2020), and with a protracted migration history, the chosen national context allows for the investigation of distinctions and commonalities between first and second generation migrants.

Additionally, highly skilled employees in Germany often have a migration background, further making Germany an ideal location for our investigative purposes.

Through a systematic qualitative analysis of 130 semi-structured interviews with highly skilled migrants of the first and second generation, this study provides an in-depth and nuanced understanding of different forms of cultural identities and the impact of these identities on the migrants' cross-cultural and cross-lingual bridging skills. More specifically, regarding the migrants' cultural identity, we found differences between first and second generation highly qualified migrants, but also within generations. On this basis, we differentiate within the first generation of migrants between those who primarily have an ethnic identity *("anchored migrants")*, and those with a split identity *("torn migrants")*; similarly, we separate within the second generation of migrants between those with a plural identity *("adaptive migrants")*, and those with a mainstream identity *("reborn migrants")*. Linking subsequently cultural identities with cross-cultural and cross-lingual bridging skills, we found that *adaptive migrants* are in the best position to develop highly sought-after bridging skills due to their dual embeddedness in their ethnic and mainstream contexts. On this basis, by combining cultural identity with cross-cultural and cross-lingual bridging skills and by focusing on generational differences, our investigation advances research on (highly skilled) migrants and their valuable skills with which they contribute to the effective management of MNCs.

4.2   Theoretical Background

4.2.1   Migrants' acculturation processes

International migration is an undeniable reality of today's societies. Circumstances such as armed conflict, political injustice and dictatorship, economic disparities, career and family reunion motives, or getting a higher education determine millions of people to pursue international relocation. The global number of individuals who have pursued international relocation has steadily increased over years, leading to a peak of 272 million migrants in 2019 (UN, 2020).

Migrants bring to their receiving countries their traditions, ways of thinking and languages (Sayad, 1998). As a result, their lives might continue to be determined by their ethnic cultural and linguistic framework, which oftentimes is inconsistent with that of the host country (Repke & Benet-Martinez, 2017; Tadmor, Galinsky & Maddux, 2012). On the other hand, the prolonged exposure to a different cultural and language system also allows migrants the possibility of experiencing new worldviews (Nguyen & Benet-Martinez, 2010). Moreover, migrants are usually faced with the challenging necessity of having to acculturate, at least partially, to this new cultural environment (Bakker, van der Zee & van Oudenhoven, 2006; Berry, 1997; Thomas, 2016). These voluntary or required adjustment processes can take place in various domains, such as language use or cultural values, which could potentially lead to cultural identity change (Bakker et al., 2006; Nguyen & Benet-Martinez, 2007; Zane & Mak, 2003).

Various factors seem to play a role in migrants' acculturation towards the respective mainstream society, such as race (Fernández, 1996; Navarrete & Jenkins, 2011), gender (Crul & Vermeulen, 2003), or reason to migrate (Nguyen & Benet-Martinez, 2010). Of particular relevance appears to be the educational level (Berry, 1997; Polek, van Oudenhoven & ten Berge, 2008). Low qualified migrants, who usually come from low social strata (Crul & Doomernik, 2003; Thomson & Crul, 2007), often undertake in their receiving countries unskilled jobs in manufacturing or construction (Portes & Fernandes-Kelly, 2008). Their primary concern is mostly to find a more secure and economically improved situation (Cook, Dwyer & Waite, 2011). By contrast, highly qualified migrants, i.e. those who hold at least a tertiary education degree, move to another country more likely with the intention to permanently stay (Hajro, Zilinskaite & Stahl, 2017). Moreover, higher education has been found to be associated with better acculturation towards the host culture (Polek et al., 2008).

For conceptual clarity, it appears important to differentiate between the acculturation processes of migrants and of (organizational and self-initiated) expatriates. Both constructs have consistently been used interchangeably (Al Ariss, 2010), leading to an unclear differentiation between them (Al Ariss & Crowley-Henry, 2013; Guo & Al Ariss, 2015). Both, expatriates and highly qualified migrants, usually possess higher educational degrees and go through a relocation process. *Organizational expatriates* decide to relocate mainly for career development reasons within a particular organization and are expected to fulfil certain functions in one of the organization's foreign subsidiaries (Zikic, 2015). The duration of their stay in the receiving country is contractually limited (Nguyen & Benet-Martinez, 2010) to usually two to four years (Dickmann & Harris, 2005; Konopaske & Werner, 2005). Due to the limited amount of time they spent in their receiving country, organizational expatriates tend to limit their acculturation towards their mainstream society to the level of social exchanges (Searle & Ward, 1990).

By contrast, *self-initiated expatriates* have more personal than career-oriented motivations to relocate and they do not enjoy the support of an organization. However, by contrast to migrants, self-initiated expatriates have a more temporary relocation mindset, planning to either return to their country-of-origin or move on to a third country (Agullo & Egawa, 2009; Cerdin & Selmer, 2014; Tharenou, 2010). Even if self-initiated expatriates stay longer than organizational expatriates in their receiving country, on average they tend to relocate after a decade (Tharenou, 2015). As such, they are likely to keep a strong connection to their ethnic values and norms while temporarily adapting to the mainstream culture (Cerdin et al., 2014).

By contrast, migrants often have a combination of career-related and personal reasons for their relocation (Zikic, 2015) and they usually have a more permanent mindset regarding their stay in their receiving countries (Al Ariss & Crowley-Henry, 2015; Cerdin et al.,2014; Cerdin & Selmer, 2014; Nguyen & Benet-Martinez, 2010). Due to the most likely permanent stay in their receiving country, migrants tend to see the mainstream country as their new, permanent home, identify with its culture and seek, if and when possible, its citizenship (Tharenou & Kulik, 2020). Thus, migrants are more likely to choose a more encompassing, comprehensive psychological acculturation towards their mainstream societies, which also involves a change in norms and values (Simon & Ruhs, 2008). However, these phenomena have hardly been investigated given that international management research has focused more on organizational or self-initiated expatriates, thus overlooking migrants, whereas the migration literature has been interested more in macro-level issues, for example the consequences of brain drain on sending economies, thus neglecting micro-level phenomena, such as migrants' acculturation processes and ensuing cultural identity formation (Al Ariss & Syed, 2011; Hajro et al., 2017).

4.2.2 Migrants' cultural identity

The formation of cultural identity is closely linked to (behavioral) acculturation (Vora, Martin, Fitzsimmons, Pekerti, Lakshman & Raheem, 2019). Cultural identity can be defined as the individual perception of oneself in relation to certain cultural communities (Berry & Sabatier, 2010). When developing a cultural identity, individuals embrace a particular worldview and engage in certain practices which tie them to a specific society (Miller & Collette, 2019). While initial studies asserted that migrants exchange one cultural identity for the other (Alba & Nee, 1997; Berry, 2003; Rumbaut, 1997), current conceptions hold that migrants can internalize multiple cultures (Eytan, Jene-Petschen & Gex-Fabry, 2007). Therefore, the cultural identity of migrants is believed to be determined by two main factors: the degree to which they identify with the ethnic culture (i.e., the country-of-origin), and the degree to which they develop a mainstream identity (i.e., the receiving country) (Berry & Sabatier, 2010).

Furthermore, we argue that migrants' cultural identity is impacted by generational dynamics, as identity related mental frames are formed through an individual's upbringing (Erikson, 1963; Erikson, 1966). These frames can become so strongly imbedded that a change will not easily take place anymore (Ringberg, Odekerken-Schröder & Christensen, 2007). For this reason, we are interested in this study in investigating the differences between the identity formation of the first and second generation migrants. First generation migrants were born outside of their receiving country and have obtained mainstream citizenship through naturalization (Algan, Dustmann, Glitz & Manning., 2010). Because first generation migrants change national contexts at a later point in life, they tend to mainly identify with their ethnic country (Fitzsimmons, 2013; Gong, 2007). In comparison, second-generation migrants are the offspring of first generation migrants, and were born and raised in the mainstream society (Heath, Rothon & Kilpi, 2008; Worbs, 2003). Thus, second generation migrants are most likely to have multiple identity constructs, due to the strong dual influence of their parents and of the society into which they were born (Luna, Ringberg & Perrachio, 2008). It is generally believed that it can take up to three generations until migrants develop mainly mainstream identities (Fitzsimmons, 2013).

Language is one of the strongest symbols of cultural attachment and a carrier of discourse (Schneider, Fokkema, Matias, Stojcic, Ugrina & Vera-Larrucea, 2012). Due to its social function, host language proficiency has often been considered in migration research as a pertinent indicator of mainstream acculturation (Nguyen & Ahmadpanah, 2014; Ward & Kennedy, 1993). Conversely, ethnic language proficiency has often been investigated in relation to the preservation of ethnic heritage (Yagmur & van de Vijver, 2012). The differentiation between first and second generation migrants pertaining to their language skills is usually described as follows: first generation migrants grow up with their ethnic language and, while subsequently learning the mainstream language, tend to keep the ethnic language dominant (Waters & Jimenez, 2005), whereas the second generation usually grows up bilingually, i.e. are proficient in both the mainstream and the ethnic languages (Fitzsimmons, 2013).

The acculturation process of migrants towards their receiving culture is multidimensional, encompassing cultural knowledge, language proficiency (Nguyen & Benet-Martinez, 2007) and ultimately even changes in identity (Bakker et al., 2006; Birman, 1994; Eytan et al., 2007; Gordon, 1964). In spite of these complexities, migration studies have mainly focused on migrants' ethnic identity, often paying less attention to migrants' identification with the mainstream society or even plural forms of identification (Sabatier, 2008).

Since migrants with high educational levels tend not only to better appropriate the receiving country's language (Yagmur & van der Vijver, 2012) but also to develop more often high levels of identification with the mainstream society (Recchi & Nebe, 2003), we found it imperative to take this educational distinction into consideration. Most of the initial literature on migration (e.g. Algan et al., 2010; Simon & Ruhs, 2008; Söhn, 2008; Vedder, Sam & Liebkind, 2007) has focused on unskilled migrants and their (often problematic) integration into their receiving countries. Topics such as the educational shortfalls of the second generation (Crul & Doomernik, 2003; Phalet & Swyngedouw, 2003; Vedder et al., 2007) or their high levels of unemployment (Westin, 2003) have often been the focus of migration studies, mostly leaving the economically successful migrants of both the first and the second generation unexplored. We thus intend to address this shortcoming in our study.

4.2.3 Migrants' cross-cultural and cross-lingual bridging skills

Receiving societies have frequently been described as benefiting from highly qualified migrants as they fill in shortages of skilled workforce, thus boosting economic growth (Shirmohammadi, Beigi & Stewart, 2019). In addition, employers can take advantage of certain cultural and language skills which migrants, particularly highly skilled ones, possess. These skills are highly sought after by multinational organizations, due to the critical cultural and linguistic challenges they face in their international operations. For example, cultural diversity can lead to problems in maintaining team collaboration and agreement (Hong, 2010). A teams' cultural heterogeneity can therefore result in conflicts, which usually are resolved at the expense of the minority group (Amaram, 2007). Furthermore, language diversity can impede the personal interaction between different organizational members or stakeholders (Sekiguchi, 2016).

These are examples for problematic instances, where highly qualified migrants can step in and engage in bridging activities between actors of different cultures and languages. In doing so, they can assist with international work processes and business operations (Backmann et al., 2020), ultimately improving their outcomes. Highly qualified migrants are therefore particularly suitable in navigating across the problematic cultural and language faultlines of international business operations (Dau, 2016; Fitzsimmons, Miska & Stahl, 2011), solving miscommunications (Nguyen & Benet-Martinez, 2010), and becoming skilled cultural mediators. As a result, they are considered an important part of the global talent pool of multinational companies (Guo & Al Ariss, 2015), making them highly valuable in the context of international business operations (Cohen, Kassis-Henderson & Lecomte, 2015).

Because migrants live at an intercultural crossroad (Bierbrauer & Klinger, 2005), their cultural identities play a salient role in the bridging activities they undertake (Sekiguchi, 2016). In order to increase our understanding of how migrants can contribute to their international workplaces, it is therefore essential to investigate how they organize their identity patterns (Fitzsimmons, 2013). On this basis, we explore how different identity patters of first and second generation migrants can influence their cross-cultural and -lingual bridging skills at the workplace (Vora et al., 2019). Despite the relevance of these bridging skills, research about highly qualified migrants and their employment in international business operations has remained scarce (Benson-Rea & Rawlinson, 2003; Guo & Al Ariss, 2015). If anything, research investigated how highly qualified migrants manage to join attractive employers, however leaving out their professional experiences once recruited (Tharenou & Kulik, 2020). Taking these unexplored issues into consideration, we intend to investigate *how the first and the second generation of highly qualified migrants differ in the impact of their cultural identity on their cross-cultural and cross-lingual bridging skills.*

4.3 Methodology

4.3.1 Research design

As we intended to gain a deeper understanding of the interplay between cultural identity, and cross-cultural and cross-lingual bridging skills of first and second generation migrants with the intention of new theory building (Buckley, 2002; Van Maanen, 1979), we found an explorative, inductive research approach to be most appropriate. We thus sought to collect detailed information about first-hand experiences pertaining to cultural identities and bridging skills (Corley, 2015), focusing in particular on the "who" (specifically, first and second generation highly qualified migrants), "how" (specifically, cross-cultural and cross-lingual bridging skills) and "why" aspects (specifically, due to their cultural identity) (Doz, 2011). Contextualizing our data according to generational differences greatly helped us to explain what otherwise might have been regarded as inconsistencies (Gligor, Esmark & Gölgeci, 2016).

We started our study based on more general information from cross-cultural management research and migration research regarding cultural identity and cross-cultural and -lingual bridging skills. Iterating between our interview data and the literature prompted us to extend our lines of investigation to new ones, which we had previously not taken into consideration (Edmondson & McManus, 2007). For example, after various rounds of data collection and data analysis and more focused further literature revisions, we were able to inductively uncover and explain patterns *within* and *between* generations of migrants regarding the impact of cultural identity on bridging activities and ultimately develop our systematization model.

4.3.2   Research setting

Differences in institutional settings such as labor market regulations or welfare systems can substantially influence migration processes (Geddes & Balch 2002; Recchi & Nebe, 2003). In order to avoid the moderation of our findings by divergent national migration systems, we decided to keep the receiving country context consistent and conducted our study on highly qualified migrants living and working in Germany. Due to significant protracted migration inflows, we consider Germany to be an ideal research setting, particularly given our focus on generational differences. Ever since the first major wave of immigration of the so-called "guest workers" in the 1950s, Germany has continuously attracted many migrants from multiple countries and cultures. As a result, currently about 26% of Germany's population has a migration background (Bundeszentrale für politische Bildung, 2020). This continuous and by now long-lasting influx of migrants enabled us to investigate developments over more than one generation. Furthermore, due to Germany's export-oriented economy, German companies' operations are highly international, making cross-cultural and cross-lingual exchanges frequent and critical. These exchanges can easily be adversely impacted by communication problems, misunderstandings or misconceptions (Tenzer, Pudelko & Harzing, 2014). Consequently, cross-cultural and cross-lingual bridging skills of highly qualified migrant employees are of strategic relevance as they can contribute to the effective functioning of these international business exchanges.

Given our specific research purposes, we had several sampling criteria. First, we followed the principles of theoretical sampling by searching for informants whose specific characteristics allowed us to uncover associations which formed the building blocks of our conceptualization efforts (Glaser & Strauss, 1967). We particularly looked for highly qualified first and second generation migrant employees working for multinational companies. For this, we referred to the stage development theory. Since identity is a fundamental component of our research purposes and since identity is usually formed during adolescence (Erikson, 1966), we drew the generational line between the first and second generation at adolescence, i.e. individuals who migrated to Germany after adolescence were categorized as first generation migrants, while those who migrated before, during adolescence, or were the offspring of first-generation migrants, were categorized as second generation migrants. Furthermore, since it takes an average of five years to develop cross-cultural skills (Hong, 2010), we selected only first generation migrants who had lived and worked in Germany for at least five years. While keeping the receiving country (Germany) constant, we sought migrants from a large variety of countries of origins, thus including a wide array of ethnic cultures and languages to increase the robustness of our findings (Miles & Huberman, 1994) when juxtaposing the experiences of migrants from first and second generation. The first interviewees were contacted though personal networks (the first author of this study herself has a migration background in Germany) or social media platforms such as LinkedIn, Xing, and Facebook. Afterwards, a snowball sampling was adopted, in which already interviewed individuals enabled contact with further potential interviewees.

Overall, our interviewees came from 47 countries (Table 1). We also covered a wide range of industries and functional areas our respondents worked in (Table 2 and Table 3). This diversity on various dimensions facilitated a contextualized investigation of phenomena relevant to us from multiple angles, thereby broadening and deepening our spectrum of understanding and theory generation (Eisenhardt & Graebner, 2007).

Table 1. Generational status and ethnic background of interviewees

Generational status	Ethnic background (countries)	Number of interviews
First generation	Argentina, Australia, Bolivia, Brazil, China, Colombia, Croatia, France, Hungary, India, Iran, Italy, Lithuania, Mexico, Netherlands, Pakistan, Palestine, Peru, Poland, Romania, Russia, Senegal, South Africa, Spain, Taiwan, Thailand, Turkey, United Kingdom, United States of America, Venezuela.	58
Second generation	Algeria, Argentina, Bosnia, Brazil, Bulgaria, Canada, China, Croatia, France, Greece, Italy, India, Kazakhstan, Lebanon, Mexico, Palestine, Peru, Philippines, Poland, Romania, Russia, Serbia, Slovakia, South Africa, South Korea, Sri Lanka, Sweden, Turkey, United Kingdom, United States of America, Vietnam.	72

Table 2. Interviewees according to their employers' industries

Industry	Number of interviews
Aerospace	1
Automotive producer	14
Automotive supplier	26
Bank	7
Car sharing	2
Construction	1
Consulting	5
Energy	1
Exhibition planning	1
Fashion	8
Floriculture	1
Food processing	1
Healthcare	4
Hotel	1
Household entertainment technology	1
Household products	2

Table 3. Interviewees according to their functional areas

Functional area	Number of interviews
Accounting	2
Business Analysis	13
Architecture	1
Assistance	15
CEO	1
Consulting	1
Controlling	2
Customer care/service	8
Data management	1
Design	1
Distribution	1
Division management	2
Human resources	7
IT	4
Logistics	1
Executive management	1

Industrial and mechanical engineering	7	Marketing	3
Insurance	2	Product and business development	1
Medical services	8	Product engineering	36
Music apparel	1	Product management	1
No industry mention	3	Purchasing	8
Pharmacology	4	Quality management and sales	1
Professional training	2	Regulatory	1
Real estate	2	Research	4
Research centre	4	Research and customer care	1
Software development	11	Research and division management	1
Technology services	2	Sales	10
Temporary employment	1	Sales and production	1
Textile	3	Software consulting	1
Transportation	2	Textile engineering	1
Wholesale	2	Product and business development	1

4.3.3 Data collection

In order to obtain in-depth information on the interplay between cultural identity and cross-cultural and cross-lingual bridging skills, we considered semi-structured and problem-centered interviews to be the most appropriate data collection method. This enabled us to gather insightful perceptions of our individuals' experiences on the same issues and contrast them against each other (Shah & Corley, 2006). At the same time, we were left with sufficient flexibility to follow up on unexpected aspects and critical incidents (Hajro & Pudelko, 2010). This way and through various iterations between data and literature, we established that cultural identity differences were significant not only between, but also within generations, something that we initially did not consider. We therefore incorporated in our later interviews questions pertaining to the antecedents of cultural identity to a greater extent. On this basis, we were also able to establish subgroups within the same generation and establish sub-group specific impacts of cultural identity on cross-cultural and -lingual bridging skills. Overall, we conducted between 2015 and 2018 a total of 130 semi-structured interviews with first and second generation highly qualified migrants.

Our interview guideline consisted of open-ended questions, which allowed us to obtain concrete and detailed accounts from our interviewees and clarify uncertainties where necessary (Witzel, 2000). Some of our questions led to information that was directly comparable with accounts from other interviewees, while other questions were designed to tease out information that was particular to each informant. The interview guideline consisted of four sections: we started out with a series of background information regarding age, nationality, generational status, years of stay in Germany (for first generation migrants only), reasons for migrating to Germany (for first generation migrants only). We then moved on to questions pertaining to their language use, cultural acculturation and cultural identity. In the following section, we addressed educational and job-related aspects such as degrees, position, tenure, and work tasks. In the final section of our semi-structured interviews, we aimed at exploring, among others, the use of cultural and language bridging activities at work. Samples of questions from this section include "What advantages do you have from your ethnic background at work?", "How often do you use your native language/your parents' language at work?", or "How do you improve the work with the foreign/ethnic subsidiaries?". We specifically asked our respondents on a continuous basis to provide concrete examples to support more general statements. Furthermore, we remained open towards potential emerging themes throughout the entire data collection process (Myers, 2008).

A substantial number of interviews was conducted by the first author. Being a highly qualified migrant herself, she could capitalize on her migration experience and her multicultural and multilingual background, allowing her to empathize more with her interviewees. As a result, the respondents felt free to provide rich accounts of their experiences and to openly discuss culturally and linguistically challenging situations at the workplace. In order to achieve investigator triangulation, 69 interviews were conducted by a total of 13 master students. Before conducting their interviews, the students were thoroughly prepared by the first author in a research seminar which was tailored towards this particular research project. Interviews were conducted in one of four languages, depending on the choice of preference of the interviewees: German, English, Spanish, or Romanian. All interviews were recorded and subsequently transcribed in the original language of the interview to maintain contextual authenticity (Bell & Bryman, 2007; Squires, 2009). By contrast, coding was done only in English and quotations reported in this paper were translated into English if necessary and marked accordingly.

4.3.4   Data analysis

Our inductive and qualitative research approach allowed for analyzing and theorizing during data collection (Patton, 2002). For this purpose, the qualitative data analysis program Atlas.ti was used. In the data analysis process, we sought to identify recurring patterns and connections between the phenomena that were of interest to us (Gibson, Dunlop & Cordery, 2019). In order to alleviate researcher bias (Denzin & Lincoln, 1998; Yeung, 1995), the 13 master students coded the 69 interviews they had conducted, while the first author coded the 61 interviews she led. Although the coders generally agreed on the interpretation of similar events, the labelling of codes were at times divergent. In these instances, codes were extensively discussed in multiple coding sessions among the coders and integrated to achieve consistency. Due to the various iterations between the definition, comparison and integration of codes, traditional interrater reliability measures are impossible to establish (Ladge, Clair & Greenberg, 2012). Nevertheless, the rigor of our integrated data analysis processes that comprised the input of various researchers should alleviate any concerns about bias.

We employed in this early phase of our data analysis open coding, also described as "the process of breaking down, examining, comparing, conceptualizing, and categorizing data" (Strauss & Corbin, 1990: 61). Our codes were consequently mostly taken directly from the data, thereby remaining close to our respondents' perceptions and wording (Gioia, Corley & Hamilton, 2013). For example, the quotes "I am actually a German" and "I feel German because I integrated so well here" were labelled with the code "Identifies as German". In other instances, we employed already existing theoretical constructs to arrive at our codes. Thus, quotes such as "I was always more sure about my German abilities than on my Romanian ones" and "I sometimes have difficulties finding the right words in English [ethnic language]" were labelled as "deficient ethnic language proficiency". We provide more examples for representative quotes and resulting first order codes in Table 4.

Table 4. Quotes from the interviews and first order codes

Examples of interview quotations	First order concepts
I am actually a German (second generation, Turkey, 04092015, TR)	
	Identifies as German
I actually see myself more German than Vietnamese…because I have the German mindset. (second generation, Vietnam, 13052015, TR)	
I sometimes have issues with some technical German words, but it is manageable (first generation, India, 25022016)	
At work I need more time to express myself than my colleague who are native German speakers (first generation, Spain, 22042018, TR)	Issues with mainstream language

I sometimes forget some words in English and then I think "of course, this is the word that I am missing" (second generation, South Africa, 29032016) — Deficient ethnic language proficiency

I would definetely say that I have a better command of German than of Turkish (second generation, Turkey, 16022016, TR)

As a next step, in order to reduce the number of first order codes to a feasible number (Gioia et al., 2013) and make more conceptual sense out of them, we applied the constant comparative method (Glaser & Strauss, 1967). This allowed us to remain sensitive to the data while at the same time identifying similarities and dissimilarities, enabling the creation of conceptual groupings (Glaser & Strauss, 1967). By iteratively moving back and forth between different sections of data, our conceptualization gradually emerged (Strauss & Corbin, 1990). At this stage of our data analysis, we employed axial coding, which is defined as a "set of procedures whereby data are put back together in new ways after open coding, by making connections between categories" (Straus & Corbin, 1990:6). This step facilitated further systematic reflection about the studied experiences. For this, we consolidated our first order codes into second order codes. For example, the codes "identifies as German-Kazach" and "identifies as German-Turkish" were aggregated into the second order code "Mainstream-ethnic identity".

We continuously switched back and forth between existing literature and our data, and we ultimately aggregated our second order codes into conceptual building blocks (Lee & Lee, 1999; Myers, 2008). At this stage, we contrasted the first and the second generation highly qualified migrants, paying particular attention to commonalities and differences *between* but also *within* generations. Our emerging data were continuously processed until a saturation point was reached and no further codes or new insights could be retrieved from the data (Glaser & Strauss, 1967). Following Gioia et al. (2013), we visualized our data structure (Figure 1).

Figure 1. Examples of first order codes, second order codes and conceptual building blocks

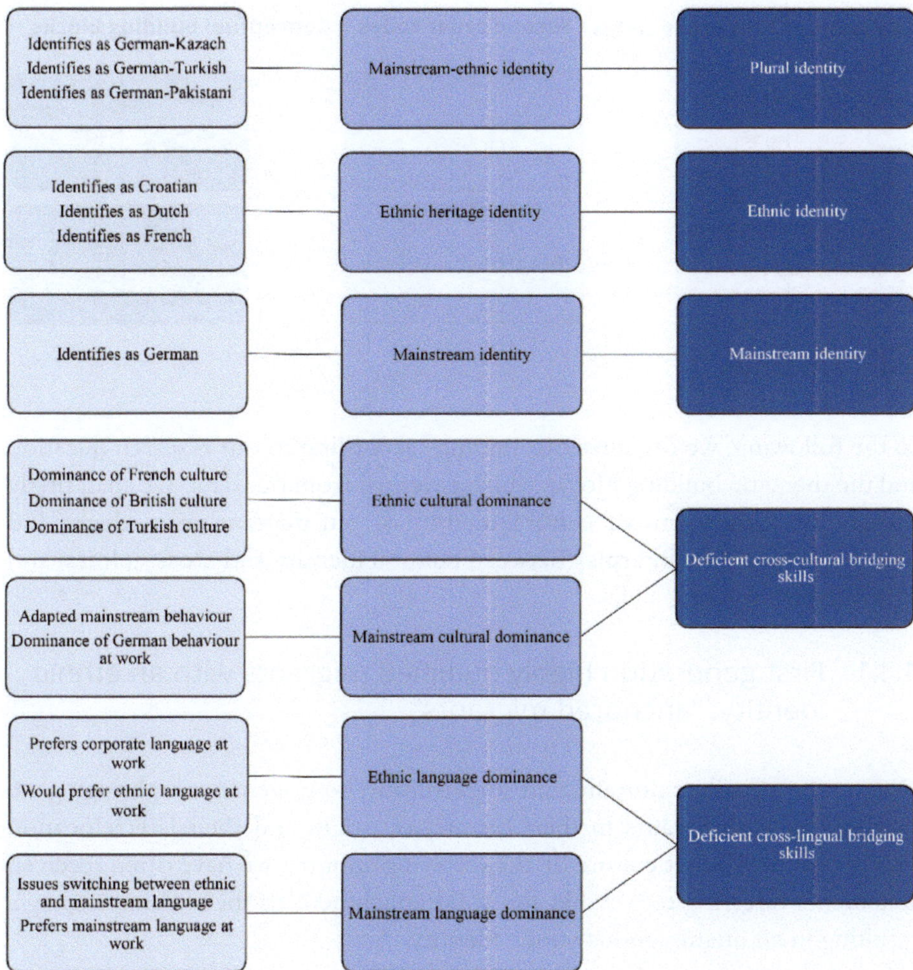

Figure 1. Examples of first order codes, second order codes and conceptual building blocks (continued)

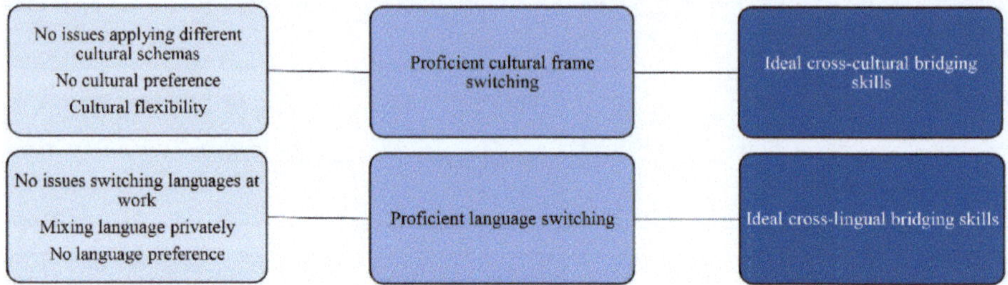

4.4　Findings

In the following, we organize our findings according to our research question and the thematic building blocks which emerged from our data. We shall firstly explore the main forms of cultural identity of our migrant respondents, and then move on to the interplay between cultural identity and cross-cultural and cross-lingual bridging skills.

4.4.1　First generation highly qualified migrants with an ethnic identity: "anchored migrants"

Due to the usually culturally and linguistically homogeneous upbringing of first generation migrants in their country-of-origin and their late relocation process to the distinct culture of the receiving country, we have often received statements referring to a stable and solid attachment to their ethnic heritage, resulting in an unambiguous ethnic identity.

I am a true Bolivian. (first generation, Bolivia, 08312017, TR)

I still identify as Hungarian. I am proud to be Hungarian and I will remain a proud Hungarian. (first generation, Hungary, 01252018, TR)

This ethnic identity orientation is in line with the stage theory of identity development (Erikson, 1963), which holds that identity is mainly achieved during adolescence, respectively young adulthood. Due to their late relocation, first generation migrants' cultural identity is dominated by their ethnic background, resulting in low identity plurality (Fitzsimmons, 2013). The first generation migrants' strong connection with their ethnic culture is evident within the private sphere but also shows within the professional sphere:

> It is a delight to work with Mexico. The mentality, the customs, the ability to understand local jokes, these are all aspects which make the difference. I enjoy working with Mexico not only because of the language, but also because of the shared mentality. I feel like a fish in the sea when I talk or negotiate with them. This is the background which I can neither deny nor cut out. (first generation, Mexico, 10022018, TR)

Due to this strong orientation towards ethnic conventions, we refer to these first generation migrants as being *anchored* in their ethnic cultures.

Furthermore, because of their highly embedded ethnic cultural knowledge, *anchored migrants* have the ability to efficiently undertake certain cultural bridging activities at work. They are able to accurately interpret ethnic business codes of conduct and, on this basis, assist colleagues from the mainstream culture on an inter-personal level in avoiding cross-cultural misunderstandings.

> I now attend much more often video conferences with the office in [city in Poland] because we came to realize that Germans are not able to read the behaviour of our Polish colleagues. For example, we gather suggestions for improvement from all foreign subsidiaries. In Poland nobody would make such a suggestion. Germans cannot understand why Polish colleagues do not make any suggestions for improvement or change. This is because the relations with the German headquarters are like that one has with the supervisor: one does not criticize or question. You can come up with your own solutions, but you will never

officially say that something must be improved. (first generation, Poland, 09262016, TR)

Our findings thus confirm, specifically for *anchored migrants,* previous findings in that migrants are proficient in their ethnic culture (Kane & Levina, 2017) and that they can use this knowledge to explain behavioral differences in the context of international collaborations (Dau, 2016; Fitzsimmons et al., 2011) to their mainstream culture colleagues.

Furthermore, we could establish that *anchored migrants* can use their ethnic cultural competencies also on the organizational level to create more stable networks between headquarters in the mainstream country and subsidiaries in their ethnic countries.

> When I have difficulties, I reach out to them [Colombian subsidiary]. And because we already have this relationship, they will help me easier rather than if I never would have cultivated this relationship. (first generation, Colombia, 09212018, TR)

Again, our findings confirm, specifically for *anchored migrants,* previous findings which established that a shared cultural background enables migrants to create deeper and more stable professional networks (Koser & Salt, 1997; Yagi & Kleinberg, 2011), thus facilitating knowledge exchange (Barner-Rasmussen, Ehrnrooth, Koveshinikov, & Mäkelä, 2010) and reducing cross-cultural conflicts (Jehn & Mannix, 2001).

Despite these clear advantages, we also observed certain limitations to the cross-cultural bridging skills of *anchored migrants.* While they were able to explain to their colleagues from the mainstream culture the behavior of business partners or subsidiary employees from their own ethnic country, they were less able to properly embrace mainstream work processes. Because their work behaviour and mentality were highly embedded in their ethnic heritage, their collaboration with mainstream colleagues was at times hampered.

> I did not grow up here…so I just do whatever I have to do [at work] and at some point, I notice that I am doing something differently

(laughs) from everyone else. And then somebody who is really close to me would tell me "Oh, you know, normally we would do it the other way in Germany." (first generation, Taiwan, 09282018)

They [Germans] try to solve things in a very standardized manner. They should try to take a different perspective…I always try to see the bigger picture, while my colleagues have a standardized work process. Like "this and that, there are rules which should be followed". Rules also exist in Italy, but one can also go around them (laughs). (first generation, Italy, 05052916, TR)

Thus, the *anchored migrants'* ability to explain cultural values, norms and behaviors is rather one-sided. As a consequence, their ability to build cultural bridges within international business operations is equally asymmetrical. This makes *anchored migrants* less than perfect cultural bridging agents. Due to this imbalance between mainstream and ethnic cultural competencies, we propose the following:

Proposition 1a:
First generation highly qualified migrants with an ethnic identity ("anchored migrants") have one-sided cultural bridging skills.

In addition to ethnic cultural knowledge, first generation migrants are, as native speakers, fully proficient in their ethnic language. The use of their ethnic language skills can facilitate a more open collaboration between team members on the inter-personal level or between mainstream headquarters and subsidiaries in their country-of-origin on the inter-organizational level:

When having phone-calls or when something complicated must be explained, I make it easier for our partners in Brazil and switch to Portuguese. (first generation, Brazil, 09272018, TR)

By sharing the same speech conventions, first generation migrants have the possibility of sensing hidden meanings in messages from ethnic subsidiaries, and therefore improve the information transfer process:

> I was directly responsible for Romania, and I could notice a certain undertone in the official mails. So I called them and asked them what was really going on. Then I found out what actually happened, and I could explain this to my supervisor. So, speaking Romanian helped me to get to the bottom of these issues more easily. I was able to interpret the information and find a solution along with my department. (first generation, Romanian, 02192016)

MNCs have consistently implemented English as a corporate language (Harzing & Pudelko, 2013) in order to manage the inherent challenges stemming from their linguistic diversity, and in the hope to facilitate communication and collaboration between international operations (Marschan-Piekkari, Welch & Welch, 1999). However, English has been proven not to be the panacea for multilingualism challenges (Aichhorn & Puck, 2017), as communication challenges persisted because of differences in English proficiency (Rogerson-Revell, 2007) or because of the difficulty in finding acceptable linguistic equivalents in a foreign language (Brannen, 2004). In addition, language barriers can also translate into issues such as lack of trust (Tenzer et al., 2014), unclear power distribution (Tenzer & Pudelko, 2017) or impeded knowledge processing (Tenzer, Pudelko & Zellmer-Bruhn, 2021) that will not simply disappear with the use of English as a business language (Marschan-Piekkari et al., 1999).

By speaking the language of their country-of-origin, our first generation *anchored* interviewees clearly indicated their ability to overcome these ingrained language barriers and improve intra-firm international collaboration and information sharing. What is more, because of their ethnic language proficiency, first generation migrants were even the preferred contact of the ethnic subsidiaries:

> They [Chinese subsidiary] also really appreciate me. They feel that they
> can communicate better with me, some of them speak Chinese with
> me every day or try to write me in Chinese every day. (first generation,
> China, 10022018)

First generation migrants' ethnic language skills were not only appreciated by local employees at the foreign subsidiary level but also by colleagues from headquarters who needed translation support:

> Translation tasks were explicitly given to me. For example, proofreading when something had to be sent to a native English speaker. Colleagues from other teams or even from other departments asked for translation support. (first generation, Australia, 07222016)

Our findings sustain previous research (Feely & Harzing, 2003) in that language bridging individuals can fulfill roles such as translators or intermediaries for those organizational members with more limited language skills. However, their language bridging function was usually not part of the *anchored* migrants' formal tasks. While some migrants might have appreciated the extra attention, others complained about the distraction that in particular translation work caused them in pursuing their actual tasks (Tenzer & Pudelko, 2017).

More importantly, similar to the issue of mainstream cultural skills, first generation migrants, in particular *achored migrants*, are highly skilled mainly when conversing in their mother tongue, respectively translating into their mother tongue, as their mainstream language skills are often not at the same proficiency level:

> Sometimes it is difficult for me to keep up at this professional level. It can happen that when translating into German, colleagues ask me what I am trying to say. In these moments, I realize that somebody who speaks German perfectly would explain things differently. But I can't always find the right words. After I explain a few times what I mean, everything is all right but in my case, it may take double the time when

> complex matters are being discussed. (first generation, Russia, 04152017, TR)

This imbalance between ethnic and mainstream language proficiency also leads to a more time-consuming communication (Hinds, Neeley & Cramton, 2014; Tenzer & Pudelko, 2016), particularly when both parties need to reach the same level of sense-making. As such, *achored migrants* have to invest a considerable amount of effort in processing the mainstream language, leaving reduced cognitive resources for firm relevant contributions in business meetings.

> I think there is room for improvement for my German and I view this as a disadvantage. If I am tired, I will not be able to concentrate anymore and follow the discussion. This is when I usually become quiet in meetings. (first generation, Turkey, 07132016, TR)

Our findings resonate with existing research (Volk, Köhler & Pudelko, 2014) in that the *achored migrants'* constant use of the mainstream language can result in cognitive overload, reducing their cognitive capacity for their main work tasks. Based on our findings, we therefore propose the following:

Proposition 1b:
First generation highly qualified migrants with an ethnic identity ("anchored migrants") have one-sided language bridging skills.

4.4.2 First generation highly qualified migrants with a segmented identity: "torn migrants"

Common conceptions pertaining to first generation migrants is that they are strongly rooted in their ethnic heritage (Fitzsimmons, 2013), as we have just described with the *achored migrants*. However, we have also had a significant amount of highly skilled first generation migrant interviewees who remained attached to their ethnic culture, while at the same time developing a new attachment to the mainstream culture.

> I would say that I have two identities... I identify a lot with Germany
> but at the same time, I also have a strong and deep connection with
> my home country, Senegal. I live in two cultures at the same time and
> in equal measure. (first generation, Senegal, 07282018, TR)

Frequently, these migrants developed a segmented identity in that they remained particularly attached to their ethnic value system in the private sphere
(relationships within family and friends) but opened themselves up to influences of the mainstream culture, mainly in the work context.

> Regarding working in Germany and how things are handled here, I
> have to say that I am more German than Latino...privately, I am more
> Latino (first generation, Argentina, 06252016, TR)

> Privately I am more Croatian and at work, I am more German. (first
> generation, Croatia, 04222015, TR)

Due to the fact that the plural form of identity that they developed was not
consistent with the manner in which they embedded the corresponding cultural traits, i.e. they separated between the professional and private sphere, we
labelled these highly skilled first generation migrants as *"torn migrants"*.

To better understand the differences between first generation migrants
who were *achored* by constrast to those who were *torn*, we compared both
groups in terms of their demographics and found that the latter group mainly
consisted of migrants who had already spent a considerable amount of time
in the mainstream society. This extended time period led to a renegotiation of
the cultural identity but only in the domain where contacts with the
mainstream culture are the most intensive, which is usually the professional
sphere. Previous studies argued that it would take a relocating individual an
average of five years to begin assimilating to the mainstream culture (Kane &
Levina, 2017). Our results seem to suggest that it lasts at least twice as long,
i.e., at least ten years, to truly renegotiate one's cultural identity and develop a
plural identity. Notwithstanding, the longer migrants stayed in the mainstream
society, the more they adapted the mainstream cultural frame in addition to

their existing ethnic cultural frame (Berg & Eckstein, 2009; Phalet & Swyngedouw, 2003).

Pertaining to their ethnic cultural skills, our respondents made unanticipated statements. Specifically, we had not received relevant input regarding the use of ethnic cultural skills at the workplace. Although first generation migrants are supposed to have proficient ethnic culture skills, it seems that our respondents who developed a plural identity form also became less comfortable in their ethnic cultural environment.

> One changes. For example, when I go to Iran, I still have contact with my former colleagues and class mates. I notice how I have changed. I think I have become more mature than them, some of their behaviour is childish for me. If I had stayed in Iran, I would have had the same opinion as them. (first generation, Iran, 06062016, TR)

> I am different, I think differently, I speak differently. Privately, I associate France a lot with vacation. I do not see Frenchmen efficient anymore. I do like it now when everything is orderly, efficient and when I see progress. This is how Germans are, Frenchmen take their fair share of time. I have difficulties when going on vacation in France to slow down. I behave German, I have been living here for too many years. (first generation, France, 02222016, TR)

The development of a new identity seems to have induced a weak attachment to their ethnic culture. This finding constasts existing research maintaining that a multicultural identity is linked to an attachment to both one's ethnic and mainstream cultures (Nyugen & Benet-Martinez, 2010). This intermediary step towards assimilation in the mainstream society led to a loss of loyalty to the culture of origin (LaFromboise, Coleman & Gerton, 1993). In light of these findings propose the following:

Proposition 2a:
First generation highly qualified migrants with a plural identity ("torn migrants")
hardly engage in culture bridging activites because they lose rapport with their eth-
nic cultures.

In spite of this loss of loyalty to their ethnic culture, the attachment to their ethnic language persisted. As such, they were able to use their ethnic language skills to improve business outcomes with ethnic clients:

> At my former employer we had French clients. My supervisor and my colleagues were all German but we had French clients. I always spoke French with them. It is advisable to speak French with Frenchmen. So for this company and for this job, my language skills were a significant advantage. (first generation, France, 02222016, TR)

Contrasting previous research that related ethnic language skills to an ethnic identification (Yagmur & van de Vijver, 2012), our first generation respondents with a plural identity maintained a linguistic connection with their ethnic heritage. This would suggest that for first generation migrants, their linguistic dominance in their ethnic language (Waters & Jimenez, 2005) remains, while their ethnic cultural internalization is eclipsed by a mainstream orientation upon a plural identity development. Nevertheless, their efficiency in language bridging was again counteracted by their insufficient mainstream language skills.

> Sometimes, when I want to express something, it is difficult to do it in German. This is why I sometimes do not feel so much at ease, I cannot express everything I want to say. I can do it in Spanish though. (first generation, Colombia, 07212016, TR)

Taking this disparity of language proficiencies into account, we propose the following:

Proposition 2b:
First generation highly qualified migrants with a plural identity ("torn migrants")
have one-sided language bridging skills.

Overall, first generation migrants seem to be highly valuable for their international employers because of their bridging activities. They are able to use their culture specific and language specific skills to explain ethnic behavioural conventions, build stable networks with ethnic business operations, improve collaboration and information transfer with ethnic subsidiaries, provide translation support or even promote better outcomes with ethnic clients. Nevertheless, while their bridging activities are solid from the ethnic side, their lack of a proficient understanding for the mainstream culture and language make them imperfect bridge makers. Furthermore, they seem to develop a plural identity upon a prolonged stay in the mainstream society (Berg & Eckstein, 2009; Phalet & Swyngedouw, 2003). Upon this process, first generation migrants strengthen their mainstream cultural orientation at the expense of the ethnic culture. Comparatively, their linguistic connection with their ethnic country remains. As a result, first generation migrants with a plural identity have even more flawed bridging abilities as they lack both a strong cultural connection with their ethnic culture and a high level of mainstream language proficiency.

4.4.3 Second generation highly qualified migrants with a plural identity: "adaptive migrants"

As we found it conceptually relevant to differentiate between generations of migrants, we focus in this second section of our findings on the identity forms and interplay between identity, and cultural and language bridging skills of second generation highly qualified migrants. In line with existing findings and conceptions regarding this second generation of migrants, we found that most of them mentioned embedding both ethnic and mainstream heritages, and therefore acknowledged having a plural identity.

> I see myself as part of both cultures. I feel German-Turkish, or Turkish-German. (second generation, Turkey, 08312017, TR)

Our findings resonate with existing research (Fitzsimmons, 2013; Fitzsimmons et al., 2017; Ward, Tseung-Wong, Szabo, Qumseya & Bhowon, 2018) that second generation migrants enjoy a multicultural upbringing and are thereby more likely to develop a plural form of identity. Furthermore, their innate multiculturalism allows them to comfortably apply either one of their cultural frames.

> It is perhaps strange to describe it but I feel both in Germany and in Mexico at home. It is as if I would slip into a different role. I signal a turn here in traffic and behave within the norms, while there [Mexico] I drive just as crazy as all the others. It is the same person actually, but each time with a different interpretation. (second generation, Mexico, 09182015, TR)

Taking this ease in switching between cultural frames and their deep double cultural internalization, we refer to these second generation migrants with a plural identity as *adaptive migrants*.

Because of their balanced cultural embeddedness, second generation migrants are also skilled at cultural bridging at the workplace. For instance, these cultural skills can be effectively used to create a stronger and more profound relation with existing ethnic clients.

> When I work with Arabs, I usually hear things such as "I feel comfortable with you, I trust you". This is crucial, even more than being an expert and being able to offer the best business conditions. The personal touch plays an even more important role in these cases. Even when there are topics which are less related to our bank, I receive requests to help out. This is when I realize that they would not do this with somebody else. None of my colleagues has the private contact information of our clients or receives requests if there are problems.

> The access to them [Arabic clients] is easier for me. (second generation, Algeria, 12192015, TR)

Furthermore, second generation migrants can employ their ethnic knowledge in order to explain ethnic business conducts, mediate the work relation between ethnic and mainstream operations, and thereby avoid misconceptions or cross-cultural conflicts.

> If you send an email to a Brazilian colleague, he will only reply when he has the full solution instead of saying "I'm working on it". And even if they are delayed, they will not tell you. They just think they have to come back to you with the full solution and they don't even give you a sign that they read your email. And then the perception of the Germans is that the Brazilians don't care. I would tell the Brazilian colleagues to at least tell that they are working on it or to let us know if they are late. That might seem obvious for someone working here. In this case it was an advantage to be able to give some hints about how to reply to emails because the Germans think you are not working on it at all. (second generation, Brazil, 16122016, TR)

Our second generation respondents with a plural identity have reached through their early cultural immersion a certain level of comfort and proficiency in both ethnic and mainstream cultures (Benet-Martinez, Lee & Leu 2006; Schwartz & Unger, 2010). The ease of applying distinct cultural frames (Hong, Morris, Chiu & Benet-Martinez, 2000) seems to be a source of competitive advantage for our second generation's employers (Zikic, 2015). We found that the balanced internalization of distinct cultural frameworks and the ability to appropriately use and interpret these allow second generation migrants with a plural identity to properly build cultural bridges between mainstream and ethnic operations. We therefore propose the following:

Proposition 3a:
Second generation highly qualified migrants with a plural identity ("adaptive migrants") are ideal cultural bridging agents.

Besides being highly proficient in their embedded cultures, second generation migrants have a double language proficiency which allows them for example to facilitate communication with ethnic clients.

> We recently received an inquiry from a Russian client. He did not speak German well and when I called him, I spoke Russian. He found it great to be called back in his mother tongue. This is with clients, and with my direct colleagues I speak German. (second generation, Russia, 07162018, TR)

It seems that when confronted with limited corporate language skills, second generation migrants can intervene and act as translators (Feely & Harzing, 2003). Building on our respodents' assertions, it seems that their ethnic language skills were highly appreciated by organizational members from ethnic business operations. As such, their ethnic language skills proved to be a source of strategic advantage (Hong & Minbaeva, 2017; Zikic, 2015) in the international communication process.

Besides facilitation of business relations with ethnic based operations, second generation migrants also use their language skills informally, in order to speed up work processes.

> For example, upon receiving documents from our Turkish business partners, we sometimes realize that they are not completely translated. We ask for an official translation but this usually takes time. I am then asked to make a translation so that our colleagues can work until the official translation arrives. I usually make it either verbally or in an e-mail. It cannot be used as an official internal document but they trust me and they rely on me because they know that I can do it. (second generation, Turkey, 04292015, TR)

Building on this, we noticed how second generation migrants seem to be at ease when switching between their ethnic and mainstream languages:

> There are no language preferences between work and home. At home we speak mainly Turkish because of mother, she has a lower level of German. At work, I speak German with German colleagues, and Turkish with Turkish colleagues. (second generation, Turkey, 07162018, TR)

Taking this linguistic dexterity and high level of command of multiple languages in consideration, we propose the following:

Proposition 3b:
Second generation highly qualified migrants with a plural identity ("adaptive migrants") are ideal language bridging agents.

Overall, the simultaneous cultural and linguistic immersion of second generation migrants (Martin & Shao, 2016; Vora et al., 2019) gives them highly proficient skills at both a cultural and a language level (Portes, 1995; Zhou, 1997), making them ideal bridging agents. Their bridging abilities are not flawed as in the case of the first generation, as they maintained a positive and strong relation with both ethnic and mainstream culture and language, resonating with the concept of multicultural assimilation (LaFromboise et al., 1993). Second generation migrants with a plural identity can therefore be highly valuable bridging agents for multinational corporations.

4.4.4 Second generation highly qualified migrants with a mainstream identity: "reborn migrants"

Although common conceptions relating to second generation migrants sustain the existence of a plural identity form, we have also had respondents of the second generation who asserted having a mainstream identity.

> I am German. I grew up here, I was born here, hence I am German. (second generation, Vietnman, 05132015, TR)

> I would definetely say that I identify as German. After all, I grew up here. Of course, one is never seen as completely German, due to the name, for example, but I would personally identify as German. (second generation, Russia, 07202016, TR)

These findings contrast with existing beliefs that it would take up to three migrant generations to reach a mainstream identity (Connor, 1974; Fitzsimmons, 2013). We wanted to gain a deeper understanding in this second generation cohort and we looked for potential commonalities. We have found that, generally those second generation migrants who had a family background with a lower social status, tended to identify more often with the mainstream society. Since our second generation respondents are mostly the offspring of the first generation low skilled guest workers, in order to enhance one's social identity, status, and self-esteem (Ashforth & Mael, 1989), second generation migrants might have adopted the mainstream identity (Bakker et al., 2006; Turner, 1987). Morevoer, due to the high educational level our second generation respondents were able to reach and their high earning positions in multinational companies, the development of a mainstream identity would resonate with existing research that upon reaching a higher socio-economic level, migrants will tend to have a stronger identification with the mainstream society (Phalet & Swyngedouw, 2003). Due to this strong identity orientation towards the mainstream society, in spite of their multicultural upbringing, we refer to these second generation migrants as *reborn migrants*.

Similar to the first generation migrants with a plural identity form, the assimilation process of our second generation respondents who adopted the mainstream identity led to a significant loss of attachment towards their parents' cultural heritage (LaFromboise et al., 1993). As a result, we did not receive relevant input pertaining to their potential cultural bridging skills. Given their inherent simultaneous immersion in their ethnic and mainstream cultures (Martin & Shao, 2016), we believe that not the lack of cultural knowledge, but the emotional detachment and lack of internalization of the ethnic heritage hindered their cultural bridging skills. Following this, we propose the following:

Proposition 4a:
Second generation highly qualified migrants with a mainstream identity ("reborn migrants") rarely engage in cultural bridging activities due to an ethnic cultural detachment.

In spite of the absence of an internal ethnic cultural frame, second generation migrants seem to be highly proficient in both ethnic and mainstream languages. They were thus able to use their language skills to create better relations to ethnic clients. Nevertheless, these language bridging tasks were usually performed spontaneously and irregularly.

> We have Turkish clients and I speak to them Turkish if I realize that their German is insufficient or when their children are not around to translate. (second generation, Turkey, 09262015, TR)

Language studies suggest that an inequality in language fluency and proficiency can lead to less information sharing and damages rapport building (Haas & Cummings, 2015; Neeley, Hinds & Cramton, 2012). Second generation migrants are proficient multilinguals (Waters & Jimenez, 2005) and by employing these skills, they are able to act as efficient language bridging agents. Even more so, they seem to have hardly any difficulties in employing their languages in various job related situations, showing a high level of proficiency in bridging from both linguistic sides, ethnic and mainstream. Nevertheless, it seems that these reborn migrants do not perform such language bridging activities on a regular basis and their skills are certainly not always imbedded in their job tasks.

> I was not asked to perform certain tasks because of my background. We had Spanish suppliers but I did not oversee those products. I never thought of it actually, it never happened. (second generation, Bolivia, 08312017, TR)

Taking this lack of synergy between highly proficient ethnic and mainstream language skills on the one side, and organizational supporting tasks on the other side, we propose the following:

Proposition 4b:
Second generation highly qualified migrants with a mainstream identity ("reborn migrants") irregularly fulfil language bridging activities.

Overall, second generation migrants' innate knowledge, skills and switching abilities allow them to create a stronger business relation with ethnic business operations, facilitate international communication, avoid misunderstandings stemming from differences in business behaviours, or speed up work processes. Nevertheless, the identity development process influences the fulfilment of these bridging activities. According to our findings, second generation migrants with a plural identity can act as ideal cultural and language adaptive migrants. Their cultural bridging and language bridging abilities are superior to those of the first generation because of their internalization of both ethnic and mainstream cultures and languages. On the other hand, second generation migrants with a mainstream identity seem to be alienated from their ethnic culture but keep a high working proficiency in their ethnic and mainstream languages. As a result, they generally do not engage in cultural bridging activities but have the linguistic potential to effectively fulfil language bridging activities. However, their language bridging activities are strained by the lack of overlap between skills, job tasks, and willingness to perform language bridging activities on a regular basis.

Upon our research efforts, we obtained four building blocks pertaining to identity and eight regarding the cultural and language bridging skills, which constitute the basis for our modelling. For eight of these blocks we have developed propositions, which we would like to put forward in our subsequent model (Figure 2).

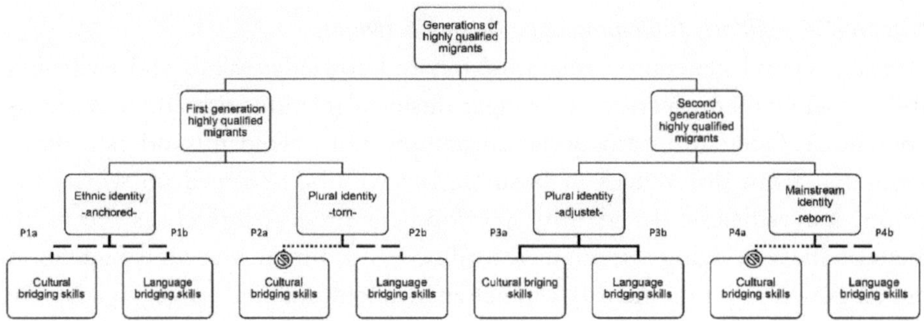

FIGURE 2. The impact of migrants' identity on cultural and language bridging skills

4.5 Discussion

Our study lies at the intersection of two research streams: (international) migration and cross-cultural management. By focusing on highly skilled migrants and drawing a differentiating line between the first and second migrant generation, we were able to provide a fine-grained depiction of the interlink between their adopted identities and the cultural bridging and language bridging activities they performed in an international work context. Our study advances and contrasts existing research, thereby providing a more balanced and comprehensive understanding on the identity development of migrant generations, and their indispensable cultural and language skills in a globalized business world.

4.5.1 Theoretical implications

Most of previous migration studies have mainly focused on unskilled or low skilled migrants, and their (often problematic) integration in their receiving societies or their educational struggles (e.g. Algan et al., 2010; Simon & Ruhs, 2008; Söhn, 2008; Vedder et al., 2007). Moreover, existing migration research has focused on these integration issues mainly at macro-contextual levels, often relating them to immigration policies (Guo & Al Ariss, 2015). As a result, the individual level has been left mostly unexplored (Hajro et al., 2017). Due to this imbalance, the understanding of highly skilled migrants' individual experiences or challenges has remained widely overlooked in the migration literature (Al Ariss, 2010; Al Ariss et al., 2012; Kofman & Raghuram, 2006). Furthermore, although highly qualified migrants have cultural and language skills which can be useful for international business operations, the use of their skills have hardly been noticed or addressed (Benson-Rea & Rawlinson, 2003).

4.5.1.1 *Contributions to the migration literature*

By employing an explorative, inductive approach, we were able to give individual voice to highly qualified migrants and generate a more systematic understanding of their identity and bridging-related experiences. We have therefore responded to the call for more research relating to this well-educated relocating workforce (Al Ariss, 2010; Al Ariss, et al., 2012). For this, we firstly differentiated conceptually between first and second generation highly qualified migrants due to their different upbringing in terms of culture and language. By engaging in an explorative study, we conducted a fine-grained investigation both *between* and *within* generations of highly skilled migrants. Established beliefs from previous studies convey that first generation migrants usually remain oriented towards their ethnic culture, while second generation migrants are able to develop plural forms of identity (Fitzsimmons, 2013), encompassing their multiple cultures and languages. Correspondingly, most of our first generation respondents asserted having an ethnic identity. Nevertheless, contrasting existing conceptions about first generation migrants, we have found that the development of a plural identity for first generation migrants is possible. Upon a closer examination, we noticed that the length of residence plays a significant role in the process of plural identity formation. To be more specific, with a significant increase of the duration of their stay in the mainstream society, first generation highly qualified migrants were more likely to develop a plural identity.

While most of our second generation respondents conferred having a plural identity, we have also had a certain share of second generation migrants who identified mainly with the mainstream society. Due to the exploratory nature of our study, we were able to single out the commonalities between these respondents. We were thus able to ascertain that the social status of a second generation migrant's family mediates the development of a mainstream identity. Specifically, second generation migrants whose families had a low social status tended to adopt a mainstream identity. Our second generation migrants were usually the offspring of the first waves of low qualified guest workers who migrated in order to fill in the shortage of blue collar workers. This second generation offspring was able to reach higher educational levels and an according higher social level in the mainstream society. Our findings are in line with existing research conveying that with the advancement of one's socio-economic status, migrants will adopt more often a mainstream identity (Phalet & Swyngedouw, 2003; Recchi & Nebe, 2003).

4.5.1.2 Contributions to the cross-cultural management literature

Highly qualified migrants usually fill in the shortage of skilled human resources (Al Ariss & Syed, 2011), and their cultural and language abilities can prove to be an invaluable addition to the talent pool of multinational companies (Hong & Minbaeva, 2017). Building on the forms their identities took, we further looked into the cultural and language bridging skills of highly qualified migrants. First generation migrants with an ethnic identity possessed solid ethnic culture and language skills. Their strong orientation towards their ethnic heritage resonates well with their ethnic upbringing and change of a cultural context at a later point in life. Nevertheless, their cultural bridging and language bridging skills are overshadowed by their lack of a proficient understanding and internalization of the mainstream culture and language. By comparison, first generation migrants with a plural identity had even more flawed cultural bridging and language bridging skills. Upon the development of a plural form of identity, first generation migrants seem to detach themselves from their ethnic culture. Due to their ethnic upbringing, we convey that not the lack of ethnic cultural knowledge, but the loss of a deep attachment to their ethnic culture hinders their cultural bridging activities. Nevertheless, first generation migrants with a plural identity seem to have kept a linguistic connection with their ethnic heritage. In spite of this, it is their insufficient mainstream language knowledge, which again makes them less suitable language bridging agents.

We further investigated the culture bridging and language bridging abilities of second generation highly qualified migrants. Due to their multicultural and multilingual upbringing, most of our second generation respondents asserted having a plural identity. Their innate multiculturalism and multilingualism (Martin & Shao, 2016; Portes & Zhou, 1993) gave them a well-balanced proficiency in both ethnic and mainstream culture and language. Therefore, they are able to act as ideal cultural bridging and language bridging agents. Last but not least, we explored the bridging activities of second generation migrants with a mainstream identity. Similar to first generation migrants with a plural identity, second generation migrants with a mainstream identity did not internalize their ethnic cultures. Due to their culturally mixed upbringing, we believe that not a lack of ethnic cultural knowledge, but the lost connection with their ethnic heritage impeded their cultural bridging activities. Moreover, they were proficient in their ethnic language, but they did not engage in regular language bridging activities, since these were not embedded in their job tasks and they sometimes viewed them as a diverging task, which they fulfilled only when circumstances dictated.

Overall, based on our existing findings, we convey that second generation migrants with a plural identity fulfil best the role of cultural bridging and language bridging agents, due to their ingrained balanced but proficient internalization of ethnic and mainstream cultures and languages. Second generation migrants with a mainstream identity are culturally estranged from their ethnic heritage, in spite of their language proficiencies. By comparison, first generation migrants, regardless of their ethnic or plural identity, do not have a balanced cultural internalization or mainstream language proficiency. This makes both first generation migrants, and second generation migrants with a mainstream identity imperfect cultural and language bridging agents.

4.5.2 Managerial implications

The cultural and linguistic diversity of internationally operating companies has led to multiple business challenges (Earley & Mosakowski, 2000; Stahl & Tung, 2015). In order to counteract these challenges, various solutions have been implemented, nonetheless with mixed results (Kostova & Roth, 2003). One of the much more novel answers to these issues is the employment of individuals who have the necessary skills and knowledge to act as bridging agents within international business operations. For this, highly qualified migrants can prove to be remarkably valuable human resources (Cohen et al., 2015; Nguyen & Benet-Martinez, 2010). They have much better knowledge of their ethnic culture and language than their mainstream colleagues, enabling them better exchanges with ethnic stakeholders of their international employers (Kane & Levina, 2017). Their knowledge and abilities can help them build bridges between mainstream and ethnic operations.

Due to the fact that some second generation migrants maintained that they did not use their ethnic knowledge and skills because of a lack of synergy between tasks and skills, we encourage human resource managers and supervisors to give more weight during employment decisions to the existing soft skills of highly qualified migrants, create support mechanisms for the implementation of their skills, and even look more for synergies between job tasks and cultural and language backgrounds. The first step towards embedding the skills of highly qualified migrants in international operations is by acknowledging the potential of their cultural and language skills. Regrettably, in spite of being a fast-growing demographic, migrants still remain an "under-appreciated resource for international organizations" (Fitzsimmons et al., 2017: 63).

Moreover, although second generation highly qualified migrants do possess ideal cultural bridging and language bridging skills, our findings also show a sub-category of second generation individuals who have a superficial rapport to and internalization of their ethnic heritage. This in turn impacts their ability and willingness to use their skills. In order to effectively use the embedded skills of second generation highly qualified migrants, we encourage managers to also take into account, up to a certain degree, bridging tasks preferences of their employees. By doing so, a more pertinent overlap between tasks and skills could be insured, which in turn can positively impact the functioning of international operations (Thomas, 2016; Zanoni, Janssens, Benschop & Nkomo, 2010).

We furthermore consider it imperative that managers also develop tolerance for low proficiencies in the mainstream culture and/or mainstream language. Our results show that first generation highly qualified migrants still struggle with the lack of mainstream cultural internalization or a flawed proficiency in the mainstream language. This imbalance in cultural and language proficiencies is quite justifiable, given their late relocation process. For this, first generation highly qualified migrants could receive company support in improvement opportunities for their mainstream language skills in order to avoid time-consuming information exchange or a cognitive burden.

4.5.3 Limitations and suggestions for future research

We acknowledge that our study presents certain limitations which in turn can provide the basis for future research. First, in order to avoid the complexities stemming from contextual differences and institutional frameworks, we have opted to conduct our research in the same mainstream country, i.e. Germany. This also enabled us to keep the receiving country's culture and language frames constant, thus avoiding potential pitfalls stemming from different mainstream adaptation strategies or challenges. Future research could fruitfully extend our line of research by conducting their investigation in other contextual frames. The different immigration or integration policies and mainstream culture and language could yield different results pertaining to migrant identity development and employment.

Secondly, due to the abundance of factors which influence the decision to migrate (e.g. educational, work related, family), we have decided to look into the individual experiences of highly qualified migrants. Since the decision to relocate plays a salient role in the adaptation to one's receiving country (Nguyen & Benet-Martinez, 2010), we have chosen to conduct our study solely on migrants in order to avoid a potential moderation of our results. We therefore acknowledge that different relocating categories (e.g. trailing spouses, refugees, asylum seekers) might go through distinct new identity formation processes.

Furthermore, their reactions to the experiences they make in their receiving countries could also differ from our highly qualified migrants. We thus encourage future studies to also look into other relocating categories since their adaptation processes could yield intriguing new outcomes.

Last but not least, the use of cultural and language skills in bridging activities is related to individual job tasks. We have had migrant respondents who did not fulfil these activities either due to the lack of overlap between skills and job tasks, or because they viewed them as a distracting activity, or because they even willingly withdrew from having much contact with their ethnic culture. We subsequently encourage future researchers to further investigate the motivation of migrants to use their skills and knowledge at the workplace. This would render an even more accurate portrayal of the experiences and use of migrants' skills, thus bringing existing research to a new level of understanding.

4.6 Conclusion

Our study advances the understanding on a mainly understudied relocating group of individuals. We therefore respond to the calls for a more thorough individual investigation of highly qualified migrants' experiences in their receiving countries and their skills. We found that identities can change *within* generations of migrants and that the development of a new identity can mediate their cultural and language bridging skills and activities. We thus highlight the importance of taking the generational and identity feature of highly qualified migrants into account upon investigating their valuable cultural and language bridging skills. We encourage a more complex conceptualizations of migrants' adaptation processes to their receiving countries and the subsequent development of cross-cultural and language skills.

4.7 Bibliography

Aichhorn, N., & Puck, J. (2017). "I just don't feel comfortable speaking English": Foreign language anxiety as a catalyst for spoken-language barriers in MNCs. *International Business Review*, 26(4): 749-763.

Agullo, B., Egawa, M. 2009. International careers of Indian workers in Tokyo: Examination and future directions. *Career Development International*, 14 (2): 148-168.

Al Ariss, A. (2010). Modes of engagement: migration, self-initiated expatriation, and career development. *Career Development International*, 15(4): 338-358.

Al Ariss, A., Cascio, W. F., & Paauwe, J. (2014). Talent management: Current theories and future research directions. *Journal of World Business*, 49(2): 173-179.

Al Ariss, A., & Crowley-Henry, M. (2013). Self-initiated expatriation and migration in the management literature: Present theorizations and future research directions. *Career Development International*, 18(1): 78-96.

Al Ariss, A., & Özbilgin, M. (2010). Understanding self-initiated expatriates: Career experiences of Lebanese self-initiated expatriates in France. *Thunderbird International Business Review*, 52(4): 275-285.

Al Ariss, A., & Syed, J. (2011). Capital mobilization of skilled migrants: A relational perspective. *British Journal of Management*, 22(2): 286-304.

Al Ariss, A., Koall, I., Ozbilgin, M., & Suutari, V.. (2012). Careers of skilled migrants: towards a theoretical and methodological expansion. *Journal of Management Development* 31(2): 92-101.

Alba, R., & Nee, V. (1997). Rethinking assimilation theory for a new era of immigration. *International Migration Review*, *31*(4): 826-874.

Algan, Y., C. Dustmann, A. Glitz, & A. Manning. (2010). The economic situation of first and second-generation immigrants in France, Germany and the United Kingdom. *Economic Journal*, 120(542): F4–F30

Amaram, D. I. (2007). Cultural diversity: Implications for workplace management. *Journal of Diversity Management (JDM)*, *2*(4), 1-6.

Ashforth, B.E., & Mael, F. (1989). Social identity theory and the organization. *Academy of Management Review*, 14(1): 20-39.

Backmann, J., Kanitz, R., Tian, A.W., Hoffmann, P., & Hoegl, M. (2020). Cultural gap bridging in multinational teams. *Journal of International Business Studies*, 51: 1283 - 1311.

Bakker, W., Van Der Zee, K., & Van Oudenhoven, J.P. (2006). Personality and Dutch emigrants' reactions to acculturation strategies. *Journal of Applied Social Psychology*, 36(12): 2864-2891.

Barkema, H.G., Bell, J.H., & Pennings, J.M. (1996). Foreign entry, cultural barriers, and learning. *Strategic Management Journal*, 17(2): 151-166.

Barner-Rasmussen, W. (2015). What do bicultural-bilinguals do in multinational corporations. In N. Holden, S. Michailova & S. Tietze (Eds). *The Routledge companion to cross-cultural management*: 142-150. London and New York: Routledge.

Barner-Rasmussen, W., Ehrnrooth, M., Koveshnikov, A., & Mäkelä, K. (2008). Kingpins of the multinational: On the characteristics and roles of boundary spanners in multinational corporations. *In 34th EIBA Conference, Tallinn* (pp. 11-13).

Barner-Rasmussen, W., Ehrnrooth, M., Koveshinikov, A., & Mäkelä, K. (2010). Linchpins of the multinational: Functions, resources and types of boundary spanners in multinational corporations. *Academy of Management Best Conference Paper Proceedings*.

Barner-Rasmussen, W., Ehrnrooth, M., Koveshnikov, A., & Mäkelä, K. (2014). Cultural and language skills as resources for boundary spanning within the MNC. *Journal of International Business Studies*, 45(7), 886-905.

Baruch, Y., Budhwar, P.S. , & Khatri, N. (2007). Brain drain: Inclination to stay abroad after studies. *Journal of World Business*, 42(1): 99-112.

Bell, E., & Bryman, A. (2007). The ethics of management research: an exploratory content analysis. *British Journal of Management*, 18(1): 63-77.

Benet-Martínez, V., Lee, F., & Leu, J. (2006). Biculturalism and cognitive complexity: Expertise in cultural representations. *Journal of Cross-Cultural Psychology*, 37(4): 386-407.

Benson-Rea, M., & Rawlinson, S. (2003). Highly skilled and business migrants: Information processes and settlement outcomes. *International Migration*, 41(2): 59-79.

Berg, M.L., & Eckstein, S. (2009). Introduction: Reimagining migrant generations. *Diaspora: A Journal of Transnational Studies*, 18(1): 1-23.

Berry, J. W. (2003). Conceptual approaches to acculturation. In K. M. Chun, P. B. Organista, & G. Marín (Eds.), *Acculturation: Advances in theory, measurement, and applied research:* 17-37. Washington, DC: American Psychological Association.

Berry, J.W. (1997). Lead article: Immigration, acculturation, and adaptation. *Applied Psychology: An International Review*, 46(1): 5-68.

Berry, J.W., & Sabatier, C. (2010). Acculturation, discrimination, and adaptation among second generation immigrant youth in Montreal and Paris. *International Journal of Intercultural Relations*, 34(3): 191-207.

Bierbrauer, G., & Klinger, E.W. (2005). The influence of conflict context characteristics on conflict regulation preferences of immigrants. *Journal of Cross-Cultural Psychology*, 36(3): 340-354.

Birman, D. (1994). Acculturation and human diversity in a multicultural society. In E. J. Trickett, R. J.Watts, & D. Birman (Eds.), *Human diversity: Perspectives on people in context*: 261-284. San Francisco: Jossey-Bass.

Brannen, M.Y. (2004). When Mickey loses face: Recontextualization, semantic fit, and the semiotics of foreignness. *Academy of Management Review*, 29(4): 593-616.

Brannen, M. Y., Garcia, D., & Thomas, D. C. (2009). Biculturals as natural bridges for intercultural communication and collaboration. In *Proceedings of the 2009 international Workshop on Intercultural Collaboration* (pp. 207-210).

Buckley, P. J. (2002). Is the international business research agenda running out of steam? *Journal of International Business Studies*, 33(2): 365–373.

Bundeszentrale für politische Bildung. (2020). *Bevölkerung mit Migrationshintergrund I*. Available at: https://www.bpb.de/nachschlagen/zahlen-und-fakten/soziale-situation-in-deutschland/61646/migrationshintergrund-i. [Accessed 31 December 2020].

Cerdin, J.L., Diné, M.A., & Brewster, C. (2014). Qualified immigrants' success: Exploring the motivation to migrate and to integrate. *Journal of International Business Studies*, 45(2): 151-168.

Cerdin, J. L., & Selmer, J. (2014). Who is a self-initiated expatriate? Towards conceptual clarity of a common notion. *The International Journal of Human Resource Management, 25*(9), 1281-1301.

Cohen, L., Kassis-Henderson, J.K., & Lecomte, P. (2015). Language diversity in management education: towards a multilingual turn. In: Holden, N, Michailova, S, Tietze, S (eds) The Routledge Companion to Cross-Cultural Management: 151-160. London: Routledge.

Connor, J.W. (1974). Acculturation and family continuities in three generations of Japanese Americans. *Journal of Marriage and the Family,* 36: 159-165.

Corley, K.G. (2015). A commentary on "what grounded theory is…" engaging a phenomenon from the perspective of those living it. *Organizational Research Methods,* 18(4): 600-605.

Cook, J., Dwyer, P., & Waite, L. (2011). The experiences of accession 8 migrants in England: Motivations, work and agency. *International Migration,* 49(2): 54-79.

Crul, M., & Doomernik, J. (2003). The Turkish and Moroccan second generation in the Netherlands: Divergent trends between and polarization within the two groups. *International Migration Review,* 37(4): 1039-1064.

Crul, M., & Vermeulen, H. (2003). The second generation in Europe. *International Migration Review,* 37(4): 965-986.

Dau, L.A. (2016). Biculturalism, team performance, and cultural-faultline bridges. *Journal of International Management,* 22(1): 48-62.

Denzin, N. K., & Lincoln, Y. S. (1998). *The handbook of qualitative research.* Thousand Oaks, CA: Sage.

Dickmann, M., & Harris, H. (2005). Developing career capital for global careers: The role of international assignments. *Journal of World Business,* 40(4): 399-408.

Doz, Y. (2011). Qualitative research for international business. *Journal of International Business Studies,* 42(5): 582-590.

Earley, C.P., & Mosakowski, E. (2000). Creating hybrid team cultures: An empirical test of transnational team functioning. *Academy of Management Journal,* 43(1): 26-49.

Edmondson, A.C., & McManus, S.E. (2007). Methodological fit in management field research. *Academy of Management Review,* 32(4): 1246-1264.

Eisenhardt, K. M., & Graebner, M. E. (2007). Theory building from cases: Opportunities and challenges. *Academy of Management Journal, 50*(1), 25-32.

Erikson, E. H. (1963). *Childhood and society* (2nd ed.). New York: Norton

Erikson, E.H. (1966). The concept of identity in race relations: Notes and queries. *Daedalus*, 95(1): 145-171.

Eytan, A., Jene-Petschen, N., & Gex-Fabry, M. (2007). Bicultural identity among economical migrants from three south European countries living in Switzerland. Adaptation and validation of a new psychometric instrument. *BMC Psychiatry*, 7(1): 17.

Feely, A.J., & Harzing, A.W.(2003). Language management in multinational companies. *Cross Cultural Managemen. An International Journal*, 10(2): 37-52.

Fernández, C. A. (1996). Government classification of multiracial/multiethnic people. In M. P. P. Root (Ed.). *The multiracial experience: Racial borders as the new frontier.* Thousand Oaks, CA: Sage.

Fitzsimmons, S.R. (2013). Multicultural employees: A framework for understanding how they contribute to organizations. *Academy of Management Review*, 38(4): 525-549.

Fitzsimmons, S.R., Liao, Y., & Thomas, D.C. (2017). From crossing cultures to straddling them: An empirical examination of outcomes for multicultural employees. *Journal of International Business Studies, 48*(1): 63-89.

Fitzsimmons, S.R., Miska, C., & Stahl, G.K. (2011). Multicultural employees: Global business' untapped resource. Organizational Dynamics, 40: 199-206.

Geddes, A., & Balch, A., (2002). *The political economy of migration in an integrating Europe: Patterns, trends, lacunae and their implications.* Working Paper no. 6, University of Liverpool, PEMINT.

Gibson, C.B., Dunlop, P.D., & Cordery, J.L. (2019). Managing formalization to increase global team effectiveness and meaningfulness of work in multinational organizations. *Journal of International Business Studies*, 50(6): 1021-1052.

Gioia, D.A., Corley, K.G., & Hamilton, A.L. (2013). Seeking qualitative rigor in inductive research: Notes on the Gioia methodology. *Organizational Research Methods*, 16(1): 15-31.

Glaser, B. G., & Strauss, A. L. (1967). *The discovery of grounded theory: Strategies for qualitative research*. Chicago: Aldine.

Gligor, D.M., Esmark, C.L., & Gölgeci, I. (2016). Building international business theory: A grounded theory approach. *Journal of International Business Studies*, 47(1): 93-111.

Gong, L. (2007). Ethnic identity and identification with the majority group: Relations with national identity and self-esteem. *International Journal of Intercultural Relations*, 31(4): 503-523.

Gordon, M. M. (1964). *Assimilation in American life*. New York: Oxford University Press.

Haas, M.R., & Cummings, J.N. (2015). Barriers to knowledge seeking within MNC teams: Which differences matter most? *Journal of International Business Studies*, 46(1): 36-62.

Gregurović, S., & Župarić-Iljić, D. (2018). Comparing the incomparable? Migrant integration policies and perplexities of comparison. *International Migration*, 56(3): 105-122.

Grzymala-Kazlowska, A., & Phillimore, J. (2018). Introduction: rethinking integration. New perspectives on adaptation and settlement in the era of super-diversity. *Journal of Ethnic and Migration Studies*, 44(2): 179-196.

Guo, C., & Al Ariss, A. (2015). Human resource management of international migrants: current theories and future research. *International Journal of Human Resource Management, 26*(10), 1287-1297.

Hajro, A., & Pudelko, M., (2010). An analysis of core-competences of successful multinational team leaders. *International Journal of Cross-Cultural Management*, 10(2): 175-194.

Hajro, A., Zilinskaite, M., & Stahl, G. (2017). Acculturation of Highly-qualified Migrants: Individual Coping Strategies and Climate for Inclusion. In *Academy of management proceedings*, vol. 117: 13666. Briarcliff Manor, NY 10510: Academy of Management.

Harzing, A. W., Köster, K., & Magner, U. (2011). Babel in business: The language barrier and its solutions in the HQ-subsidiary relationship. *Journal of World Business, 46*(3), 279-287.

Harzing, A.W., & Maznevski, M. (2002). The interaction between language and culture: A test of the cultural accommodation hypothesis in seven countries. *Language and Intercultural Communication*, 2(2): 120-139.

Harzing, A.-W. & Pudelko, M. (2013). Language Competencies, Policies and Practices in Multinational Corporations: A Comprehensive Review and Comparison of Anglophone, Asian, Continental European and Nordic MNCs, *Journal of World Business*, 48, 1, 87-97.

Heath, A.F., Rothon, C., & Kilpi, E. (2008). The second generation in Western Europe: Education, unemployment, and occupational attainment. *Annual Review of Sociology*, 34: 211-235

Henderson, J.K. (2005). Language diversity in international management teams. *International Studies of Management & Organization*, 35(1): 66-82.

Hinds, P.J., Neeley, T.B., & Cramton, C.D. (2014). Language as a lightning rod: Power contests, emotion regulation, and subgroup dynamics in global teams. *Journal of International Business Studies*, 45(5): 536-561.

Hong, H.J. (2010). Bicultural competence and its impact on team effectiveness. *International Journal of Cross-Cultural Management*, 10(1). 93-120.

Hong, H.J., & Minbaeva, D.B. (2017). Multiculturals as Strategic Human Capital Resources in Multinational Enterprises. In *Academy of management proceedings*, vol. 1: 15896. Briarcliff Manor, NY 10510: Academy of Management.

Hong, Y.Y., Morris, M.W., Chiu, C.Y., & Benet-Martinez, V. (2000). Multicultural minds: A dynamic constructivist approach to culture and cognition. *American Psychologist*, 55(7): 709.

Jehn, K.A., & Mannix, E.A. (2001). The dynamic nature of conflict: A longitudinal study of intragroup conflict and group performance. *Academy of Management Journal*, 44(2): 238-251.

Kane, A.A., & Levina, N. (2017). 'Am I still one of them?': Bicultural immigrant managers navigating social identity threats when spanning global boundaries. *Journal of Management Studies*, 54(4): 540-577.

Kofman, E., & Raghuram, P. (2006). Gender and global labour migrations: Incorporating skilled workers. *Antipode*, 38(2): 282-303.

Konopaske, R., & Werner, S. (2005). US managers' willingness to accept a global assignment: do expatriate benefits and assignment length make a difference? *The International Journal of Human Resource Management*, 16(7): 1159-1175.

Korteweg, A. C. (2017). The failures of 'immigrant integration': The gendered racialized production of non-belonging. *Migration Studies*, 5(3): 428-444.

Koser, K., & Salt, J.(1997). The geography of highly skilled international migration. *International Journal of Population Geography*, 3(4): 285-303.

Kostova, T., & Roth, K. (2003). Social capital in multinational corporations and a micro-macro model of its formation. *Academy of Management Review*, 28(2): 297-317.

Ladge, J. J., Clair, J. A., & Greenberg, D. (2012). Cross-domain identity transition during liminal periods: Constructing multiple selves as professional and mother during pregnancy. *Academy of Management Journal*, 55(6): 1449-1471.

LaFromboise, T., Coleman, H.Ll, & Gerton, J. (1993). Psychological impact of biculturalism: Evidence and theory. *Psychological Bulletin*, 114(3): 395.

Lee, T.W., & Lee, T. (1999). *Using qualitative methods in organizational research.* Thousand Oaks, CA: Sage.

Liu, X., Gao, L., Lu, J., & Wei, Y. (2015). The role of highly skilled migrants in the process of inter-firm knowledge transfer across borders. *Journal of World Business*, 50(1): 56-68.

Luna, D., Ringberg, T., & Peracchio, L.A. (2008). One individual, two identities: Frame switching among biculturals. *Journal of Consumer Research*, 35(2): 279-293.

Marschan-Piekkari, R., Welch, D., & Welch, L. (1999). In the shadow: The impact of language on structure, power and communication in the multinational. *International Business Review*, 8(4): 421-440.

Martin, L., & Shao, B. (2016). Early immersive culture mixing: The key to understanding cognitive and identity differences among multiculturals. *Journal of Cross-Cultural Psychology*, 47(10): 1409-1429.

McKinsey & Company, (2019). *Globalization in Transition: The Future of Trade and Value Chains.* Available at: https://www.mckinsey.com/~/media/mckinsey/featured%20insights/innovation/globalization%20in%20transition%20the%20future%20of%20trade%20and%20value%20chains/mgiglobalization%20in%20transition-the-future-of-trade-and-value-chains-full-report.pdf. [Accessed 29 December, 2020].

Miles, M.B., & Huberman, A.M. (1994). *Qualitative data analysis: An expanded sourcebook*. Thousand Oaks, CA: Sage.

Miller, R.L., & Collette, T. (2019). Multicultural identity development: Theory and research. In Keith., K., D., (Ed.). *Cross-cultural psychology: Contemporary themes and perspectives* (2nd ed.): 509-523. Malden, MA: Wiley-Blackwell.

Myers, M. D. (2008). *Qualitative research in business and management*. Thousand Oaks, CA: Sage.

Navarrete, V., & Jenkins, S.R. (2011). Cultural homelessness, multiminority status, ethnic identity development, and self-esteem. *International Journal of Intercultural Relations*, 35(6): 791-804.

Neeley, T.B., Hinds, P.J., & Cramton, C.D. (2012). The (un) hidden turmoil of language in global collaboration. *Organizational Dynamics*, 41(3): 236-244.

Nguyen, A.M.D., & Ahmadpanah, S.S. (2014). The interplay between bicultural blending and dual language acquisition. *Journal of Cross-Cultural Psychology*, 45(8): 1215-1220.

Nguyen, A.M.D., & Benet-Martínez, V. (2007). Biculturalism unpacked: Components, measurement, individual differences, and outcomes. *Social and Personality Psychology Compass*, 1(1): 101-114.

Nguyen, A.M.D., & Benet-Martínez, V., (2010). Multicultural identity: What it is and why it matters. In Press at R. Crisp (Ed.), *The psychology of social and cultural diversity*. Hoboken, New Jersey: Wiley- Blackwell.

Patton, M.Q. (2002). Two decades of developments in qualitative inquiry: A personal, experiential perspective. *Qualitative Social Work*, 1(3): 261-283.

Pelled, L.H., Eisenhardt, K.M., & Xin, K.R. (1999). Exploring the black box: An analysis of work group diversity, conflict and performance. *Administrative Science Quarterly*, 44(1): 1-28.

Phalet, K., & Swyngedouw, M. (2003). Measuring immigrant integration: the case of Belgium. *Studi Emigrazione*, 152: 773-804.

Polek, E., van Oudenhoven, J.P., & ten Berge, J.M. (2008). Attachment styles and demographic factors as predictors of sociocultural and psychological adjustment of Eastern European immigrants in the Netherlands. *International Journal of Psychology*, 43(5): 919-928.

Portes, A. (Ed.). (1995). *The economic sociology of immigration: Essays on networks, ethnicity, and entrepreneurship.* New York: Russell Sage Foundation.

Portes, A., & Fernández-Kelly, P. (2008). No margin for error: Educational and occupational achievement among disadvantaged children of immigrants. *The Annals of the American Academy of Political and Social Science*, 620(1): 12-36.

Portes, A., & Zhou, M. (1993). The new second generation: Segmented assimilation and its variants. *The Annals of the American Academy of Political and Social Science*, 530(1): 74-96.

Pratt, M.G. (2009). From the editors: For the lack of a boilerplate: Tips on writing up (and reviewing) qualitative research. *Academy of Management Journal*, 52(5): 856-862.

Recchi, E., & Nebe, T.M. (2003). *Migration and political identity in the european union-research issues and theoretical premises.* PIONEUR Working paper no, 1: 1-23.

Repke, L., & Benet-Martínez, V.(2017). Conceptualizing the Dynamics between Bicultural Identification and Personal Social Networks. *Frontiers in Psychology*, 8:469.

Ringberg, T., Odekerken-Schröder, G., & Christensen, G.L. (2007). A cultural models approach to service recovery. *Journal of Marketing*, 71(3): 194-214.

Rogerson-Revell, P. (2007). Using English for international business: A European case study. *English for Specific Purposes*, 26(1): 103-120.

Rumbaut, R.G. (1997). Assimilation and its discontents: Between rhetoric and reality. *International Migration Review*, 31(4): 923-960.

Sabatier, C. (2008). Ethnic and national identity among second-generation immigrant adolescents in France: The role of social context and family. *Journal of Adolescence*, 31(2): 185-205.

Sayad, A. (1998). Le retour, élément constitutif de la condition de l'immigré. *Migrations Société*, 10(57): 9-45.

Shirmohammadi, M., Beigi, M., & Stewart, J. (2019). Understanding skilled migrants' employment in the host country: A multidisciplinary review and a conceptual model. *The International Journal of Human Resource Management*, 30(1): 96-121.

Schneider, J., Fokkema, T., Matias, R., Stojčić, S., Ugrina, D., & Vera-Larrucea, C. (2012). Urban belonging and intercultural relations. In Crul, M., Schneider, J., Lelie, Fr., (Eds.). *The european second generation compared*: 285-341. Amsterdam: Amsterdam University Press.

Schwartz, S.J., & Unger, J.B. (2010). Biculturalism and context: What is biculturalism, and when is it adaptive? *Human Development*, 53(1): 26-32.

Searle, W., & Ward, C. (1990). The prediction of psychological and sociocultural adjustment during cross-cultural transitions. *International Journal of Intercultural Relations*, 14(4): 449-464.

Sekiguchi, T. (2016). Bridge individuals in multinational organisations. *The Australasian Journal of Organisational Psychology*, 9: 1-4.

Shah, S.K., & Corley, K.G. (2006). Building better theory by bridging the quantitative–qualitative divide. *Journal of Management Studies*, 43(8): 1821-1835.

Simon, B., & Ruhs, D. (2008). Identity and politicization among Turkish migrants in Germany: the role of dual identification. *Journal of Personality and Social Psychology*, 95(6): 1354.

Söhn, J. (2008). Bildungsunterschiede zwischen Migrantengruppen in Deutschland: Schulabschlüsse von Aussiedlern und anderen Migranten der ersten Generation im Vergleich. *Berliner Journal für Soziologie*, 18(3): 401-431.

Squires, A. (2009). Methodological challenges in cross-language qualitative research: A research review. *International Journal of Nursing Studies*, 46(2): 277-287.

Stahl, G.K., & Tung, R.L. (2015). Towards a more balanced treatment of culture in international business studies: The need for positive cross-cultural scholarship. *Journal of International Business Studies*, 46(4): 391-414.

Statistisches Bundesamt – Destatis. (2020). *Migration und Integration*. Available online: https://www.destatis.de/DE/Themen/Gesellschaft-Umwelt/Bevoelkerung/Migration-Integration/_inhalt.html. [Accessed 22 April 2021]

Strauss, A., & Corbin, J. (1990). *Basics of qualitative research: Grounded theory procedures and techniques*. Newbury Park, CA: Sage.

Tadmor, C.T., Galinsky, A.D., & Maddux, W.W. (2012). Getting the most out of living abroad: Biculturalism and integrative complexity as key drivers of creative and professional success. *Journal of Personality and Social Psychology*, 103(3): 520.

Takano, Y., & Noda, A. (1993). A temporary decline of thinking ability during foreign language processing. *Journal of Cross-Cultural Psychology*, 24(4): 445-462.

Tenzer, H.; Pudelko, M. & Zellmer-Bruhn, M. (2021). The Impact of Language Barriers on Knowledge Processing in Multinational Teams. *Journal of World Business*, 56, 2.

Tenzer, H. & Pudelko, M. (2017). The Influence of Language Differences on Power Dynamics in Multinational Teams. *Journal of World Business*, 52, 1, 45-61.

Tenzer, H., & Pudelko, M. (2016). Media choice in multilingual virtual teams. *Journal of International Business Studies*, 47(4), pp.427-452.

Tenzer, H.; Pudelko, M. & Harzing, A.-W. (2014). The Impact of Language Barriers on Trust Formation in Multinational Teams. *Journal of International Business Studies*, 45, 5, 508–535.

Tharenou, P. (2010). Women's self-initiated expatriation as a career option and its ethical issues. *Journal of Business Ethics*, *95*(1), 73-88.

Tharenou, P. (2015). Researching expatriate types: the quest for rigorous methodological approaches. *Human Resource Management Journal*, *25*(2), 149-165.

Tharenou, P., & Kulik, C. T. (2020). Skilled migrants employed in developed, mature economies: From newcomers to organizational insiders. *Journal of Management*, *46*(6), 1156-1181.

Thomas, D. (2016). *The multicultural mind: Unleashing the hidden force for innovation in your organization*. San Francisco, CA: Berrett-Koehler Publishers.

Thomson, M., & Crul, M. (2007). The second generation in Europe and the United States: How is the transatlantic debate relevant for further research on the European second generation? *Journal of Ethnic and Migration Studies*, 33(7): 1025-1041.

Turner, J.C. (1987). *Rediscovering the social group: A self-categorization theory*. Oxford: Blackwell.

United Nations. (2020). *World Migration Report 2020*. Available at: https://www.un.org/sites/un2.un.org/files/wmr_2020.pdf. [Accessed 29 December 2020].

Van Maanen, J. (1979). Qualitative methodology. *Administrative Science Quarterly Ithaca,* 24(4): 519-671.

Vedder, P., Sam, D.L., & Liebkind, K. (2007). The acculturation and adaptation of Turkish adolescents in North-Western Europe. *Applied Development Science,* 11(3): 126-136.

Volk, S., Köhler, T., & Pudelko, M. (2014). Brain drain: The cognitive neuroscience of foreign language processing in multinational corporations. *Journal of International Business Studies,* 45(7): 862-885.

Vora, D., Martin, L., Fitzsimmons, S.R., Pekerti, A.A., Lakshman, C., & Raheem, S. (2019). Multiculturalism within individuals: A review, critique, and agenda for future research. *Journal of International Business Studies,* 50(4): 499-524.

Ward, C., & Kennedy, A. (1993). Acculturation and cross-cultural adaptation of British residents in Hong Kong. *The Journal of Social Psychology,* 133(3): 395-397.

Ward, C., Ng Tseung-Wong, C., Szabo, A., Qumseya, T., & Bhowon, U. (2018). Hybrid and alternating identity styles as strategies for managing multicultural identities. *Journal of Cross-Cultural Psychology,* 49(9): 1402-1439.

Waters, M.C., & Jiménez, T.R. (2005). Assessing immigrant assimilation: New empirical and theoretical challenges. *Annual Review of Sociology.,* 31: 105-125.

Westin, C. (2003). Young people of migrant origin in Sweden. *International Migration Review, 37*(4), 987-1010.

Witzel, A. (2000). The problem-centered interview. FQS Forum: Qualitative Sozialforschung. *Forum: Qualitative Social Research,* 1(1): 22.

Worbs, S. (2003). The second generation in Germany: Between school and labor market. *International Migration Review,* 37(4): 1011-1038.

Yagi, N., & Kleinberg, J. (2011). Boundary work: An interpretive ethnographic perspective on negotiating and leveraging cross-cultural identity. *Journal of International Business Studies,* 42(5): 629-653.

Yağmur, K., & van de Vijver, F.J. (2012). Acculturation and language orientations of Turkish immigrants in Australia, France, Germany, and the Netherlands. *Journal of Cross-Cultural Psychology,* 43(7): 1110-1130.

Yeung, H.W.C. (1995). Qualitative personal interviews in international business research: some lessons from a study of Hong Kong transnational corporations. *International Business Review*, 4(3): 313-339.

Zane, N., & Mak, W. (2003). Major approaches to the measurement of acculturation among ethnic minority populations: A content analysis and al alternative empirical strategy. In K. M. Chun, P. Balls Organista, & G. Marın (Eds.), Acculturation: Advances in theory, measurement and applied research: 39–60. Washington, DC: American Psychological Association.

Zanoni, P., Janssens, M., Benschop, Y., & Nkomo, S. (2010). Guest editorial: Unpacking diversity, grasping inequality: Rethinking difference through critical perspectives. *Organization*, 17(1): 9-29.

Zhou, M. (1997). Segmented assimilation: Issues, controversies, and recent research on the new second generation. *International Migration Review*, 31(4): 975-1008.

Zikic, J. (2015). Skilled migrants' career capital as a source of competitive advantage: Implications for strategic HRM. *The International Journal of Human Resource Management*, 26(10): 1360-1381.

5. Discussion of my specific contribution

The three PhD articles provide a more comprehensive insight into the experiences and skills of highly qualified migrants under specific consideration of generational differences. The inductive research method allowed for the exploration of 1) highly qualified migrants' discrimination perceptions, specifically regarding microaggressions in the private and professional sphere, 2) the generational differences in cultural and language skills migrants are able to apply for the benefit of the employing organization, and 3) the interplay between cultural identity and cross-cultural and cross-lingual bridging activities.

The articles expand existing migration knowledge by looking into the less researched category of highly qualified migrants. The experiences of this subcategory of migrants have rarely been investigated since research has focused more on the challenges and problematic integration of low qualified migrants. This led to a distorted and unbalanced picture for skilled migrants. Furthermore, migration research focused often on a macro-economic standpoint, leaving the individual experiences rather unexplored. The articles not only concentrated on the highly skilled, but also on their individual experiences, and thus provide a more complete insight into the realities of migration.

Besides drawing the educational distinction, the three articles focused on the differences and commonalities of generations of migrants. A generational distinction for the highly qualified migrants has rarely been drawn in the cross-cultural management literature. This distinction is imperative upon investigating the experiences of migrants, as generations fundamentally differ in their upbringing, integration process in the mainstream society, and soft skills.

The first paper provided a more comprehensive insight into the perceptions of discrimination of highly qualified migrants. By looking both into the private and the professional spheres, I teased out distinctions and commonalities between generations of migrants in terms of their perceptions of discriminatory experiences. Overall, ethnic microaggressions seem to have risen in occurrence by contrast to explicit ethnic discrimination. This first article thus shows that the educational level of migrants appears to play a significant role in how discrimination is experienced and perceived. The first article also highlights the necessity to distinguish between different educational categories of migrants when investigating their challenges in their mainstream societies.

The second article provided a more detailed insight into the skills of migrants. Cross-cultural management research mainly uses the notion of multiculturalism when investigating particular soft skills in a multinational work context. The background of multicultural individuals, however, has rarely been taken into consideration. Migrants have seldomly been considered as an individual category of multiculturals, although migration is one of the processes in which people go through intensive multicultural experiences. Moreover, due to the highly contrasting upbringing of different generations of migrants, the generational delineation was a methodological imperative. This allowed for inter-generational differences pertaining to culture and language skills to arise. Therefore, a more accurate description of the culture and language skills of migrants and how they use them in an international work context was drawn. Moreover, going beyond the common ethnic-mainstream framework, a more encompassing understanding of the culture and language skills of migrants was provided. As such, the second article contributes to the cross-cultural management literature by developing a more detailed insight into the notions of culture general and language general skills, which go beyond culture specific and language specific skills. The inductive methodological approach allowed me to disclose certain culture general and language general skills and their strategic use in cross-cultural work encounters.

The third article focused on the interlink between identity and bridging abilities of generations of highly skilled migrants. Migrants go through a much more intensive integration process than other relocating individuals. Their adaptation to the mainstream society encompasses changes in language use, behaviour and even identity. Since identity is a complex construct which takes time to develop, a change is the more challenging. The third article provides in this context a comprehensive insight into the identity of skilled migrants. Research has often portrayed migrants as exchanging one identity for the other and common interpretive frames have looked mainly at generations as a whole. By going beyond inter-generational comparisons, a more insightful overview pertaining to identity changes even within migrant generations was delivered. Furthermore, identity is believed to be a salient factor in the bridging activities multicultural individuals such as migrants undertake. By focusing on the inter-link between identity and bridging activities, the article contributes to the cross-cultural management literature by developing a much more extensive overview on the interplay between cultural identity and the cross-cultural and cross-lingual bridging activities migrants undertake.

To conclude, I investigated a broad array of topics, ranging from perceptions of discrimination to cultural and language skills, and to the impact of identity on bridging skills. I am confident that due to my rich data set and my inductive approach, my thesis advances research on highly qualified migrants in a multinational work context, specifically with regard to generational differences, by developing novel insights of conceptual and practical relevance.

6. References for the Framework of the Thesis

Aichhorn, N., & Puck, J. (2017). "I just don't feel comfortable speaking English": Foreign language anxiety as a catalyst for spoken-language barriers in MNCs. *International Business Review*, 26(4): 749-763.

Amaram, D. I. (2007). Cultural diversity: Implications for workplace management. *Journal of Diversity Management (JDM)*, 2(4), 1-6.

Backmann, J., Kanitz, R., Tian, A. W., Hoffmann, P., & Hoegl, M. (2020). Cultural gap bridging in multinational teams. *Journal of International Business Studies*, 1-29.

Benet-Martínez, V., & Haritatos, J. (2005). Bicultural identity integration (BII): Components and psychosocial antecedents. *Journal of Personality*, 73(4), 1015-1050.

Berry, D. P., & Bell, M. P. (2012). 'Expatriates': gender, race and class distinctions in international management. *Gender, Work & Organization*, 19(1), 10-28.

Berry, J. W., & Sabatier, C. (2010). Acculturation, discrimination, and adaptation among second generation immigrant youth in Montreal and Paris. *International Journal of Intercultural Relations*, 34(3), 191-207.

Binggeli, S., Dietz, J., & Krings, F. (2013). Immigrants: A forgotten minority. *Industrial and Organizational Psychology*, 6(1), 107-113.

Bobbit-Zeher, D. (2011). Institutional policies, and gender composition of workplace gender discrimination at work: Connecting gender stereotypes. *Gender & Society*, 25, 764-786.

Carlile, P. R. (2004). Transferring, translating, and transforming: An integrative framework for managing knowledge across boundaries. *Organization Science*, 15(5), 555-568.

Cohen, L., Kassis-Henderson, J., & Lecomte, P. (2015). Language diversity in management education. In N. Holden, S. Michailova & S. Tietze (Eds). *The Routledge companion to cross-cultural management*, 151. London and New York: Routledge

Denzin, N. K. (2017). *The research act: A theoretical introduction to sociological methods*. New York: Routledge.

Edmondson, A. C., & McManus, S. E. (2007). Methodological fit in management field research. *Academy of Management Review, 32*(4), 1246-1264.

Eisenhardt, K. M. (1989). Agency theory: An assessment and review. *Academy of Management Review, 14*(1), 57-74.

Eisenhardt, K. M., & Graebner, M. E. (2007). Theory building from cases: Opportunities and challenges. *The Academy of Management Journal, 50*(1), 25-32.

Fitzsimmons, S. R. (2013). Multicultural employees: A framework for understanding how they contribute to organizations. *Academy of Management Review, 38*(4), 525-549.

Gioia, D. A., Corley, K. G., & Hamilton, A. L. (2013). Seeking qualitative rigor in inductive research: Notes on the Gioia methodology. *Organizational Research Methods, 16*(1), 15-31.

Gong, L. (2007). Ethnic identity and identification with the majority group: Relations with national identity and self-esteem. *International Journal of Intercultural Relations, 31*(4), 503-523.

Hajro, A., Zilinskaite, M., & Stahl, G. (2017). Acculturation of Hhighly-qualified Migrants: Individual Coping Strategies and Climate for Inclusion. In *Academy of Management Proceedings* (Vol. 2017, No. 1, p. 13666). Briarcliff Manor, NY 10510: Academy of Management.

Hanewinkel, V. (2012). *Kurzdossier, Focus MIGRATION, Aus der Heimat in die Heimat, Die Abwanderung hochqualifizierter türkeistämmiger deutscher Staatsangehöriger in die Türkei*. Herausgeber: IMIS der Universität Osnabrück.

Hong, H. J. (2010). Bicultural competence and its impact on team effectiveness. *International Journal of Cross Cultural Management, 10*(1), 93-120.

Hong, H. J., & Doz, Y. (2013). L'Oreal masters multiculturalism. *Harvard Business Review, 91*(6), 114-118.

Hong, H. J., & Minbaeva, D. B. (2017). Multiculturals as Strategic Human Capital Resources in Multinational Enterprises. In *Academy of Management Proceedings* (Vol. 2017, No. 1, p. 15896). Briarcliff Manor, NY 10510: Academy of Management.

Iredale, R. (2001). The migration of professionals: theories and typologies. *International Migration, 39*(5), 7-26.

Kane, A. A., & Levina, N. (2017). 'Am I still one of them?': Bicultural immigrant managers navigating social identity threats when spanning global boundaries. *Journal of Management Studies, 54*(4), 540-577.

Kostova, T., & Roth, K. (2003). Social capital in multinational corporations and a micro-macro model of its formation. *Academy of management review, 28*(2), 297-317.

Locke, K. (2001). *Grounded theory in management research.* Thousand Oaks, CA: Sage Publications.

Martin, L., & Shao, B. (2016). Early immersive culture mixing: The key to understanding cognitive and identity differences among multiculturals. *Journal of Cross-Cultural Psychology, 47*(10): 1409-1429.

Merton, R. K. (1968). *Social theory and social structure.* New York: The Free Press

Myers, M. D. (2008). *Qualitative research in business and management.* Thousand Oaks, CA: Sage.

Nguyen, A. M. D., & Benet-Martínez, V. (2007). Biculturalism unpacked: Components, measurement, individual differences, and outcomes. *Social and Personality Psychology Compass, 1*(1), 101-114.

OECD (2017). *G20 global displacement and migration report trends report.* Available online: https://www.oecd.org/g20/topics/employment-and-social-policy/G20-OECD-migration.pdf [Accessed on 15 October 2018]

Polek, E., van Oudenhoven, J. P., & ten Berge, J. M. (2008). Attachment styles and demographic factors as predictors of sociocultural and psychological adjustment of Eastern European immigrants in the Netherlands. *International Journal of Psychology, 43*(5), 919-928.

Pratt, M. G. (2009). From the editors. For the lack of a boilerplate: tips on writing up (and reviewing) qualitative research. *Academy of Management Journal, 52*(5), 856–862.

Searle, W., & Ward, C. (1990). The prediction of psychological and sociocultural adjustment during cross-cultural transitions. *International Journal of Intercultural Relations*, 14(4): 449-464.

Sekiguchi, T. (2016). Bridge individuals in multinational organisations. *The Australasian Journal of Organisational Psychology*, 9: 1-4.

Simon, B., & Ruhs, D. (2008). Identity and politicization among Turkish migrants in Germany: the role of dual identification. *Journal of Personality and Social Psychology*, *95*(6), 1354.

Sprietsma, M. (2013). Discrimination in grading: Experimental evidence from primary school teachers. *Empirical economics*, *45*(1), 523-538.

Stadler, S. A. (2017). Which competence? A comparative analysis of culture-specific vs. culture-generic intercultural competence development. *Advances in Economics and Business*, *5*, 448-455.

Stahl, G.K., & Tung, R.L. (2015). Towards a more balanced treatment of culture in international business studies: The need for positive cross-cultural scholarship. *Journal of International Business Studies*, 46(4): 391-414.

Statistisches Bundesamt – Destatis. (2020). *Migration und Integration.* Available online: https://www.destatis.de/DE/Themen/Gesellschaft-Umwelt/Bevoelkerung/Migration-Integration/_inhalt.html. [Accessed 22 April 2021]

Sue, D. W., Capodilupo, C. M., Torino, G. C., Bucceri, J. M., Holder, A., Nadal, K. L., & Esquilin, M. (2007). Racial microaggressions in everyday life: implications for clinical practice. *American Psychologist*, *62*(4), 271.

Sue, D.W., Bucceri, J.M., Lin, A.I., Nadal, K.L., & Torino, G.C. (2009). Racial microaggressions and the Asian American experience. *Asian American Journal of Psychology* S (1): 88– 101.

United Nations, Department of Economic and Social Affairs, Population Division (2020). *International Migration Report 2020* (ST/ESA/SER.A/403). Available online: https://www.un.org/sites/un2.un.org/files/wmr_2020.pdf [Accessed on 22 April 2021]

Weiss, R. S. (1994). *Learning from strangers.* New York. Free Press

Witzel, A. (2000). The problem-centered interview. Forum: Qualitative Social Research, 1(1), Available online: http://www.qualitative-research.net/index.php/fqs/article/view/1132/2521, accessed 15 September 2018.

Worbs, S. (2003). The second generation in Germany: between school and labor market. *International Migration Review*, *37*(4), 1011-1038.

Zane, N., & Mak, W. (2003). Major approaches to the measurement of acculturation among ethnic minority populations: A content analysis and al alternative empirical strategy. In K. M. Chun, P. Balls Organista, & G. Marın (Eds.), Acculturation: Advances in theory, measurement and applied research: 39–60. Washington, DC: American Psychological Association.